S0-BNJ-021

A TORONTO ALBUM
Glimpses of the City That Was

MIKE FILEY

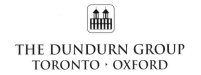

THE DUNDURN GROUP
TORONTO · OXFORD

Copyright © Mike Filey, 2001

All rights reserved. No part of this publication may be reproduced, stored in a retrieval system, or transmitted in any form or by any means, electronic, mechanical, photocopying, recording, or other- wise (except for brief passages for purposes of review) without the prior permission of Dundurn Press. Permission to photocopy should be requested from the Canadian Copyright Licensing Agency.

Publisher: Anthony Hawke
Proofreader: Natalie Barrington
Design: Jennifer Scott
Printer: Friesens

Canadian Cataloguing in Publication Data

Filey, Mike, 1941–
    A Toronto album: glimpses of the city that was

2nd ed.
ISBN 0-88882-242-1

1. Toronto (Ont.) — History — Pictorial works. I. Title.

FC3097.37.F5195 2001   971.3'54103'0222   C2001-901643-3   F1059.5.T6843F55 2001

Originally Published in 1970 by University of Toronto Press.

2   3   4   5   05   04   03

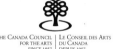

We acknowledge the support of the **Canada Council for the Arts** and the **Ontario Arts Council** for our publishing program. We also acknowledge the financial support of the **Government of Canada** through the **Book Publishing Industry Development Program** and **The Association for the Export of Canadian Books**, and the **Government of Ontario** through the **Ontario Book Publishers Tax Credit** program.

Care has been taken to trace the ownership of copyright material used in this book. The author and the publisher welcome any information enabling them to rectify any references or credit in subsequent editions.

                                    J. Kirk Howard, President

Printed and bound in Canada.⊛
Printed on recycled paper.

www.dundurn.com

Dundurn Press
8 Market Street
Suite 200
Toronto, Ontario, Canada
M5E 1M6

Dundurn Press
73 Lime Walk
Headington, Oxford,
England
OX3 7AD

Dundurn Press
2250 Military Road
Tonawanda NY
U.S.A. 14150

Preface to the 2001 Edition

When this book was first released back in the fall of 1970, I had no idea it would turn out to be such a success. Within a few months of hitting the book stores, the book made it onto several national bestseller lists. It then went through a number of reprints until the publisher simply let it go out-of-print. Now, thanks to the kindness of the original publisher, the University of Toronto Press, and the confidence of the good people at Dundurn Press, who have published many of my more recent works, *A Toronto Album: Glimpses of the City That Was* is available once again.

On a personal note, it's of particular interest to me — as I re-read what was to be the first of more than a dozen books I have written on the subject of Toronto and its past — just how much my city has changed in a brief thirty-one year period. When *A Toronto Album* first appeared, Toronto had no CN Tower, Eaton Centre, Sheraton Centre, no Scarborough Town Centre or SkyDome. Metropolitan Toronto was seventeen years old (though they were talking about outright amalgamation) and the subway system, except for extensions to the existing lines, was essentially what it is today, an unfortunate fact that in no small measure has led to the city's present-day traffic crisis.

In 1970, the Leafs' 1967 Stanley Cup victory was still a pleasant memory (and we were absolutely sure we'd do it again soon), a major league baseball team for the city was being talked about (our Jays were still seven years in the future), and the New City Hall was still just that, a new city hall, having been official-ly opened just five years earlier. And *The Toronto Sun*, for whom I still write a Sunday column, was a whole year in the future.

As for this reprint, while the pictures are the same as those in the original edition, the text has been altered slightly to reflect a few minor corrections and, I'd like to think, a better writing style that as a Chemical Technologist with the old Ontario Water Resources Commission (now part of the Ministry of the Environment) I just didn't have three decades ago.

Enjoy, again.

M.F.

Foreword

There have been many publications about Toronto, both in words and pictures, and some authors have overlooked the city's true historical character; Toronto has been portrayed as if it has only been settled since the end of the Second World War. This is because of the dynamic changes that have occurred in that period, which have made Toronto a cosmopolitan centre.

In this book, Mr. Michael Filey has illustrated some of the benchmarks and the cornerstones of Toronto's way of life and temperament — its royal celebrations, its emphasis on public transportation, public works, and a progressive, sympathetic attitude towards change.

If in one hundred years a similar book is published on "Toronto 1970," it is to be hoped that this trend and attitude will have been maintained.

I would like to commend Mr. Filey for his painstaking research in unearthing this interesting store of photographs illustrating many facets of life in Toronto through the years.

William Dennison
Mayor
City of Toronto
July 10, 1970

William Dennison served as Mayor from 1967 to 1972

Preface: To my family and friends

The purpose of this book is to present a selection of photographs that record some aspects of the city's evolution during the period 1860 to 1950. I hope that they will entertain either by stimulating among older readers their own remembrance of a city and a way of life that have all but disappeared or by showing to younger readers some glimpses of the early days of Toronto The sense of tradition, of one generation handing its systems and structures on to the next, is weak in these days of change and inter-generational gaps; it is hoped that the book will give younger Torontonians — and new Torontonians — some awareness of the city's past achievements. If we are entering an age of cities and of democratic citizenship, a knowledge of the civic past will help give us a good civic life in the future.

The photographs have been chosen for their historical value and general interest, and are generally arranged chronologically, but with some regard to topic. They depict scenes in the public theatre that is city life — mud streets and gas lamps, giant steam engines and rollicking trolley cars, favourite steamers and amusement parks. The captions have been written as accurately as possible, and are based, for the most part, on the published books and brochures listed, along with the sources of the longer quotations, at the back of the book. I am not a historian, and the work does not claim to be a balanced social history of Toronto. I hope the captions will add to the reader's understanding of the photographs and stir in him an appreciation and deeper interest in our city.

Collecting memorabilia can be very pleasant, not only through discovering a caché of old newspaper clippings at a riotous church rummage sale, but through meeting people who take an interest in one's collection, recalling with obvious enjoyment memories of their youth, such as taking a ride around the "Belt Line" or cruising the Bay on the *Bluebell*. I have met others, like myself, who are not old enough to remember a city that hasn't always been a jungle of cars, trucks, buses, and people, and who have been fascinated by these pictures of a past beyond their memory. I have enjoyed and will remember my associations with them.

It would be an impossible task to list all those who have made my research enjoyable and this book a reality. They will excuse me, I hope, if I do mention several people who have been especially helpful in the preparation of this work: Mr. Carl Banas, Mr. Rik Davidson, Mr. Allan Fleming, Mr. Scott James, and Mr. Ted Wickson. Special thanks are due also to the following organizations and people who have been kind to me during the past months: Toronto Harbour Commission, Toronto Transit Commission, City of Toronto Archives, Canadian National Exhibition and Mr. T.E. Swabey, E.L. Ruddy Company Limited, Panda-Croydon Associates and Mr. Hugh Robertson, the Marine Museum and Mr. Alan Howard.

This book would be incomplete without special mention of one person who has put up constantly with an avid, and sometimes very trying, collector: my wife.

M.F.

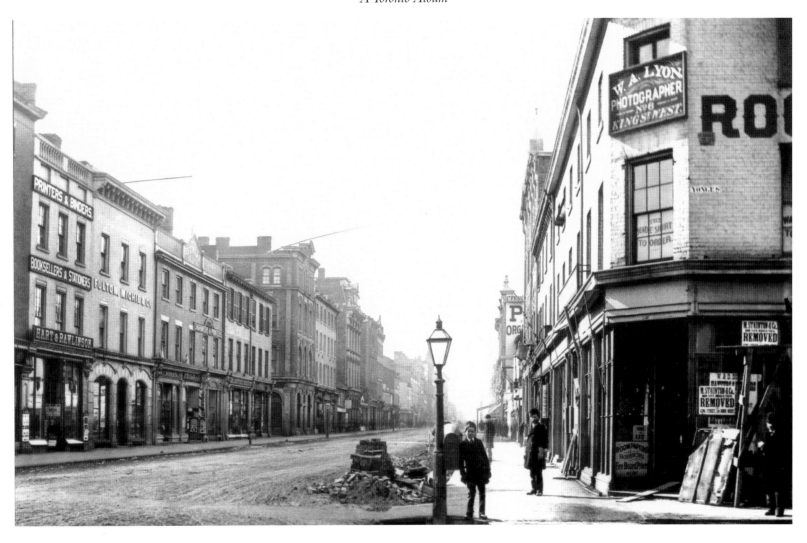

1 Looking west along King Street from Yonge, c1860

This record of life in the city of Toronto begins around 1860, because it was about that time that photographs were first taken in Toronto. The first photograph taken — of a tavern at Yonge and St. Clair — may have been by a George Thompson in 1853 on his way to Niagara. It is not always easy to give an exact date for some of these early photographs. The dates of the first three in this book, probably taken on the same day, can be deduced by the absence of streetcar tracks (laid down along King and up Yonge by September 1861), and the address given for Mr. Staunton's store in contemporary city directories.

The year 1860 can, however, be interpreted as a date of some significance in the evolution of the city. By then the forces were stirring in men's minds, down on the waterfront and elsewhere, that were to destroy much of the early classical form of the city, which we see in these photographs, leaving us today with little to recognize in them except the names of the streets. If scenes like these remind people of Georgian Dublin, a later Toronto could remind people of Belfast. This should not be surprising, since in 1850 there were more Irishmen than English, or Scots, or native Canadians, and the tendency for the mayor to be an Orangeman held for about a century.

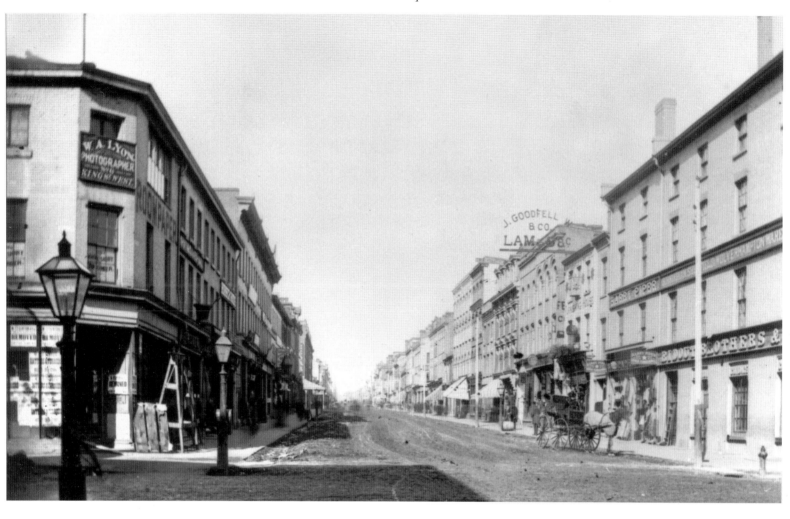

2 Looking north up Yonge Street from King, c1860

Toronto was founded in 1793 at the head of Toronto Bay, near the mouth of the Don River. To the east of the mouth of the Don lay an area of marsh, to the west a shallow shoaled harbour, practically enclosed by a long sandbar. This harbour was the reason for the original settlement and is still the prime natural resource of the city.

Roman legions would probably have recognized that first little town for what it was — a colonia, an outpost of military empire laid out in straight lines. Bounded by Berkeley and George, its main east-west axis was King Street. Its natural direction for expansion was west along King Street, and plans were made for its growth in that direction. A fire in the St. Lawrence area in 1849 and the prosperous times around 1850 produced a street lined with a variety of wholesale and retail establishments, mostly built of yellow brick. This commercial expansion affected the lower reaches of Yonge Street in the same way. Yonge was the main route to the north and much of Toronto's agricultural hinterland. By 1860, King and Yonge was Toronto's main intersection.

The carriage above is parked outside the store of Mr. Harry Piper, who later became an alderman, started Toronto's first zoo, and distributed flowers by the cartload among the poor children of his ward.

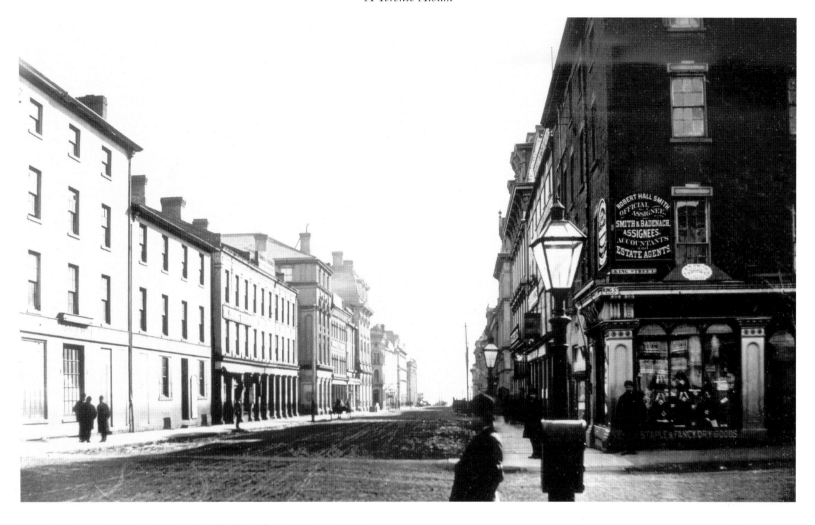

3 Looking south down Yonge to the bay from King, c1860

One can see, at the end of the street, the masts of a schooner lying in the bay, but not the train tracks, which had been recently laid along the waterfront. The streets here are still without cobbles, stones, or asphalt, though there seems to be (see *photograph 1*) a cobbled crosswalk and a pile of stones that are perhaps intended to make another across King; the sidewalks are merely planks. Under the street there were some rudimentary sewers and waterpipes. Above, there were a few overhanging signs, but the "age of wire" had also recently begun: the poles are probably carrying messages to many parts of North America (and after 1866 to Europe) in Morse code. An electromagnetic telegraph company had been formed in Toronto in 1846. Another technological improvement the city was trying to introduce was the use of manufactured gas for street lighting. Gas had been available since the early 40s, but it was still expensive. In 1861, the City Council decided to discontinue the lighting of about one half the street lamps and to have the remainder extinguished for eight nights per month during the time of moonlight.

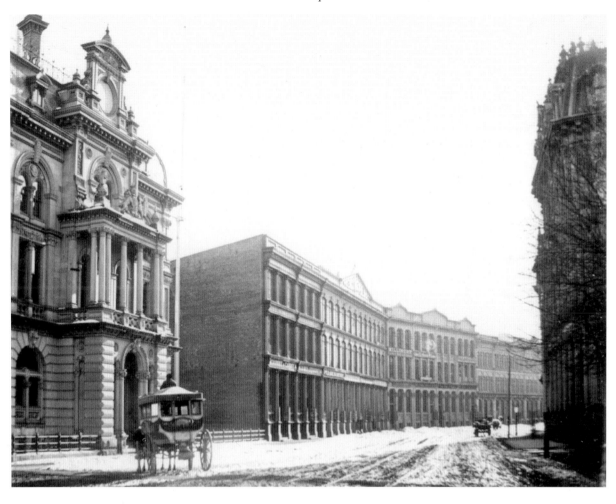

4 The south side of Front Street, looking west from Yonge, c1880

It was only in the 1850s that Toronto commerce began to be conducted in the single currency we have now. An exchange, where ownership of all sorts of goods was traded, was erected in 1855, and to facilitate credit and trade further new banks opened their doors — though others had to close theirs. Three that survived and grew were the Bank of Toronto (from 1855), the Bank of Commerce (from 1867), and the Dominion Bank (from 1871). Trust companies, insurance companies, and mortgage and loan companies opened offices to use the capital and credit accumulating in the city, and to help stabilize the ups and downs of business. By 1875 or so, Toronto had become a financial as well as a commercial centre, though still a puny rival to Montreal.

Toronto had been an alternate capital (with Quebec, Montreal, and Kingston) in the province of Canada, but in 1867 it became the full-time capital of the new province of Ontario in the new Dominion of Canada. The new dominion was also a customs union, and to Ottawa now went all the money garnered by customs and excise duties. These duties provided by far the largest source of government revenue (and continued as such until the 1930s when income tax, initially introduced during the First World War as a temporary measure, began to produce more). Its receipts were shared with the provinces. An imposing new Customs House at Yonge and Front (on the left in this photograph) was erected in 1876, symbolizing these new fiscal arrangements.

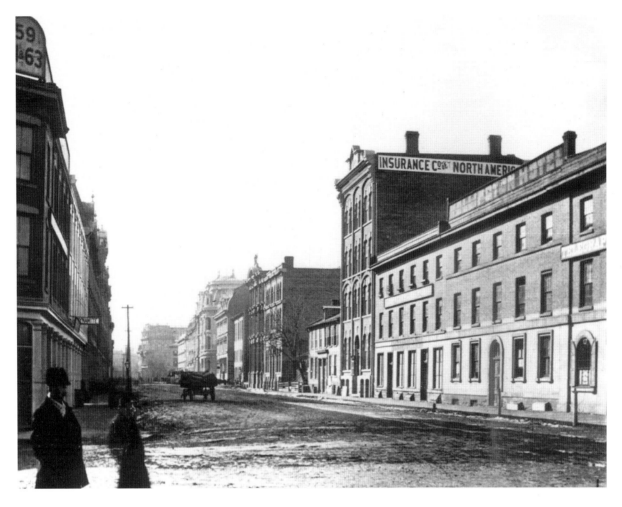

5 Looking west on Front Street from Church, 1885

Not all the city was of a noble Georgian character. The east side of York Street north of King, leading to "one of the stateliest specimens of classical architecture Canada can boast of, Osgoode Hall," was a disgrace: "dingy and rotten wooden shanties, and dens of old clothes sellers and recipients of stolen goods. There old Fagin and Moll Flanders have their lair; thither, at forbidden hours, Dick Swiveller and Thomas Idle resort for their surreptitious dram." Also on York Street was the Crompton Corset factory, the first estab- lishment in Canada to "manufacture corsets on a large scale" — 8,400 corsets a week along with hoop skirts and bustles.

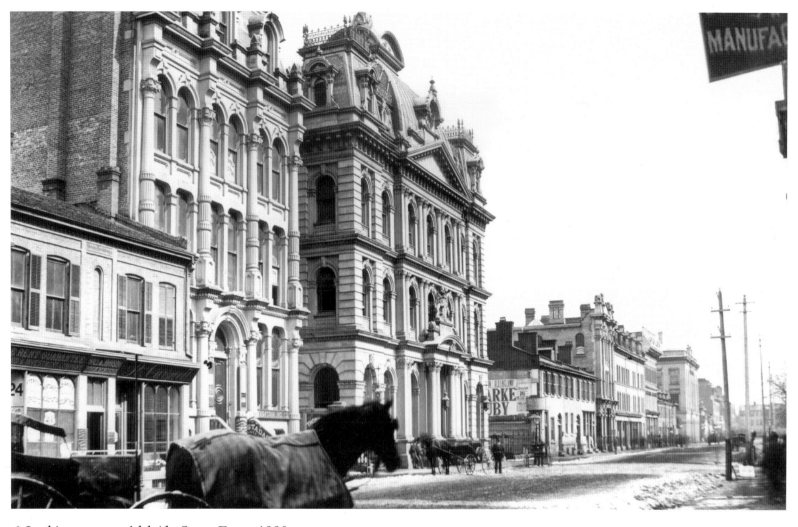

6 Looking east on Adelaide Street East, c1880

In 1867, the running of postal services had been entrusted to the federal government; in those days one of its most important functions. An impressive building in the latest romantic style — it looks now as if it could have been an opera house — was erected in 1871 as Toronto's Eighth Post Office. It was located on Adelaide Street looking down Toronto Street. Occasionally such Italian edifices could fit in well enough with the "late-flowering Georgian" style, as Eric Arthur calls it, but in the boom years after Confederation there began that process of random destruc-tion and ever larger construction which spelled the end of the order and harmony of scale that once characterized the downtown city. The effluvia of engines, steam and later internal combustion, destroyed the colour.

In the latter half of the nineteenth century, horses provided the main source of power, apart from steam engines in foundries, ships, and locomotives. Horses even propelled an early ferry, the *Peninsula Packet,* across the harbour to the "Island," as it was usually called even when it was still a peninsula; horses plodded round a windlass geared to the sidepaddles, and the vessel crossed in about forty-five minutes.

Stables were located around the St. Lawrence Market, and cartloads of hay were a common sight on the streets.

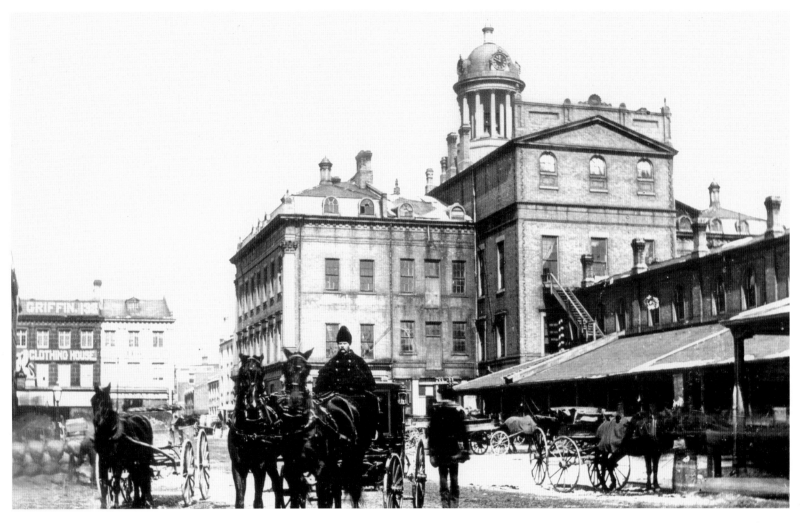

7 Looking north on West Market Street to the St. Lawrence Hall and King Street, c1875

The Police Commissioners' by-laws in regard to horse traffic included the following:

Any licensed hotel-keeper may obtain a license to run an omnibus to steamboats and railway stations, and vice versa ... [but] no licensed tavern or saloon keeper shall be entitled to a license.

No owner of any licensed cab shall drive about the streets during the day-time any notorious bad characters, or women of ill-fame.

No driver of a cab shall appear on any stand or place for hire on Sunday. No person licensed under this By-law shall abuse or ill-treat, or per-mit to be so, any horse or horses used by him.

All licensed cabs shall drive at the rate of six miles per hour at the least. No person shall gallop ...

Owners and occupants of livery stables shall not wash their horses in the streets and shall not permit more than two cartloads of manure to accu-mulate or remain at any one time between the first day of May and the first day of November.

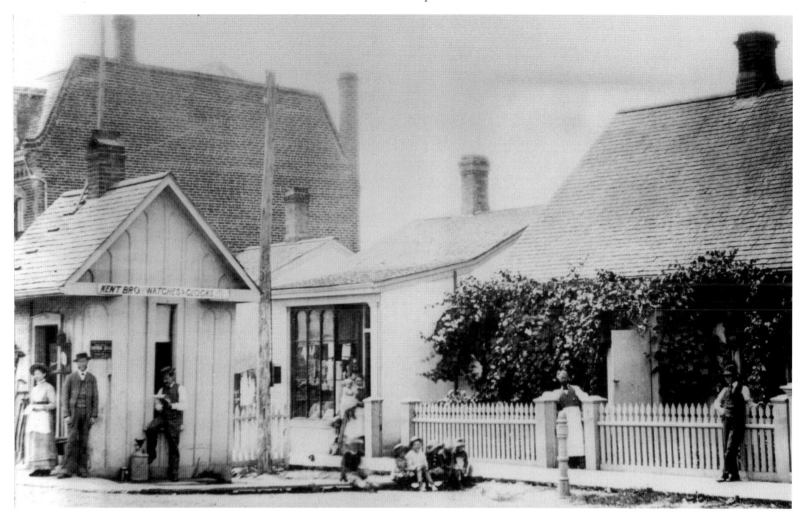

8 A Yonge Street toll house, before 1870

The city limits from 1834 to 1882 were formed, roughly speaking, by the Don River to the east, Bloor Street in the north, and Dufferin Street to the west. North of the city, Yonge Street was maintained by a turnpike trust that had six tollgates — a system that lasted until 1894. The most southerly gate had been at Bloor, but it was moved northwards, at first because the farmers it aimed to catch would dodge round by what is now Collier Street and go down to the market by Jarvis Street. It is shown here at Marlborough, just south of where the Canadian Pacific track would be laid; after 1870 it was moved further north again, halfway up the hill. Tolls varied from 10 cents for a loaded cart pulled by two horses to 1 cent for a sheep, a pig, or a goat.

Much of the area between Queen & Bloor Streets in 1834 was known as the "liberties" — land that was not fully part of the city but that the city, not the county of York, had some control over; it served to ease expansion for some forty years.

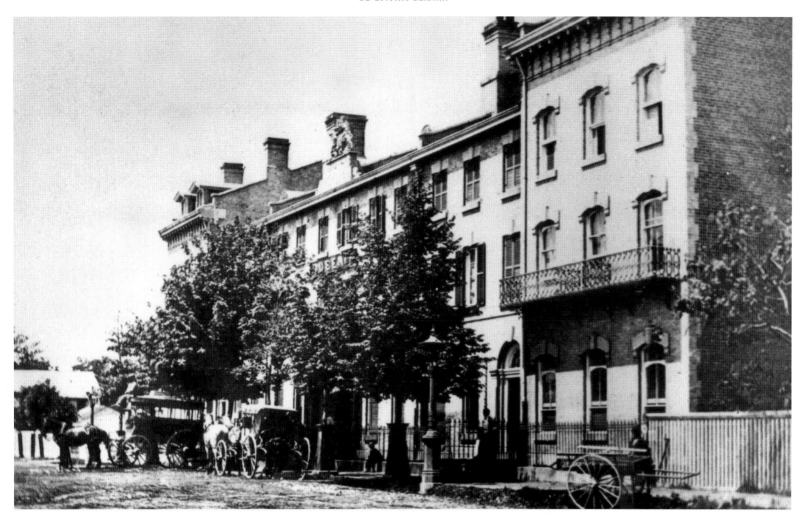

9 The Queen's Hotel in the 1860s

In 1838, there arose on the north side of Front Street, in the western outskirts of Toronto, a group of four attached townhouses called Ontario Terrace. A few years later, they housed Knox College and then, in the 1850s, became a hotel — first Sword's Hotel, then the Revere House, and then in 1862 the Queen's Hotel. "The best hotel west of New York", "an isolated island in the commercial sea of Toronto," this hotel was famed for its plush elegance, remarkable cuisine, and the cosmopolitan air it enjoyed through the patronage of visitors and tourists from royalty on down. There were frequent additions made to it, both at the sides and back as well as the top, where floors were added and a central cupola gave a grandiose touch. It was the first hotel in the country with a hot-air furnace and early on it was equipped with elevator and telephone. In the field to the east, a garden was built that boasted a fountain; in the hay field to the west circuses were held and Harry Piper opened his little zoo. By 1897, its terms for a room were (American plan) "$3.00 to $5.00 according to location." It was closed in 1927 and quickly torn down to make way for the new Royal York Hotel.

The Royal York added the prefix Fairmont in 2001 to reinforce its connection with Canadian Pacific's Fairmont chain of hotel's worldwide.

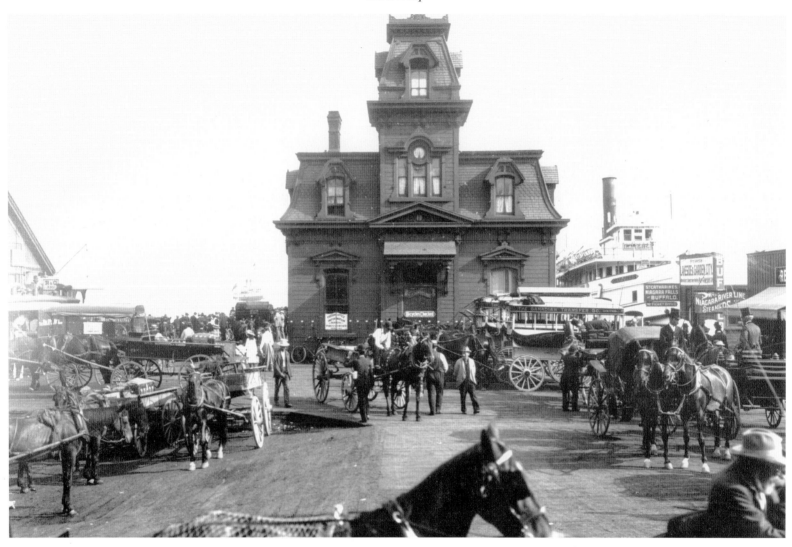

9 *Yonge Street pier at the end of the 19th century*

Road communication had always been poor and, before the railways, Toronto had looked to the harbour for the arrival and departure of most passengers and freight. Wharves, jammed with offices and warehouses, projected into the harbour; the arrival of a passenger steamer like the *Lakeside* was no doubt an exciting social affair. Right up to the turn of the century, much freight was carried around the lakes by the older wooden sailing ships or schooners seen in the next photograph.

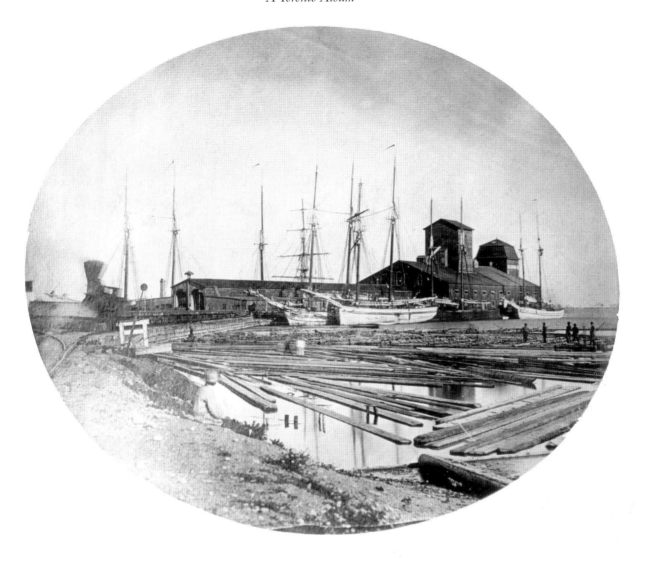

11 At the foot of Brock Street (Spadina Avenue), 1862

This photograph shows a scene typical of the Toronto waterfront for many years. A lumber raft is being assembled for towing to Quebec City. By the 1860s, logs were being hauled by rail from fifty to a hundred miles away; no longer were they floated down the Don and the Humber, for those watersheds had been denuded of this resource. In the 1880s this lumber trade came to an end, but the trade that brought the American merchantmen to this Northern Railway Company wharf would continue: they brought coal from Pennsylvania, scoured their holds, and returned home with Ontario wheat. The 1860s were the great years of Ontario's "wheating" and the grain elevator at the end for the wharf would be replaced with a larger one in 1870. Unfortunately, that was just about the time that wheat exports began to decline.

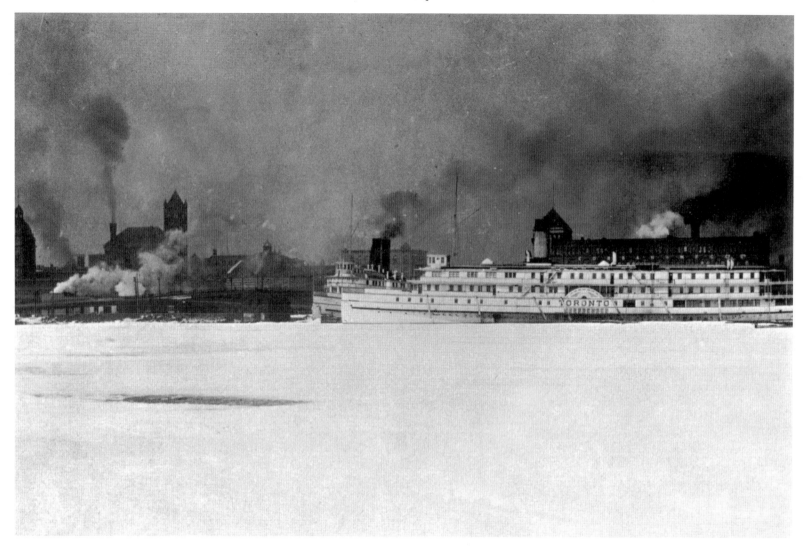

12 The lake steamer **Toronto** *icebound in the harbour, 1904*

This vessel belonged to the Richelieu and Ontario Navigation Company and carried passengers from Toronto to Rochester, Kingston, Clayton, Alexandria Bay, Brockville, and Prescott, where they could connect with ships sailing down river to Montreal and Quebec City. The company became part of the Canada Steamship Lines in 1914, at the end of a heyday of financial mergers. The service on the ships was not always appreciated: in 1891, it was asserted that "until a better lake service is provided, with increased sleeping accommodation and less necessity for a scramble at meals, the tourist had better go by train, at least to Kingston where the really enjoyable part of the trip began...." In the early years of this century, Mothersill's Seasick Remedy was advertised as "officially adopted by all Great Lake lines, (and was) guaranteed not to contain Cocaine, Morphine, Opium. It has the finest testimonials from [the] Chaplain-General of the British Forces, Lord Northcliffe, Salvation Army, etc."

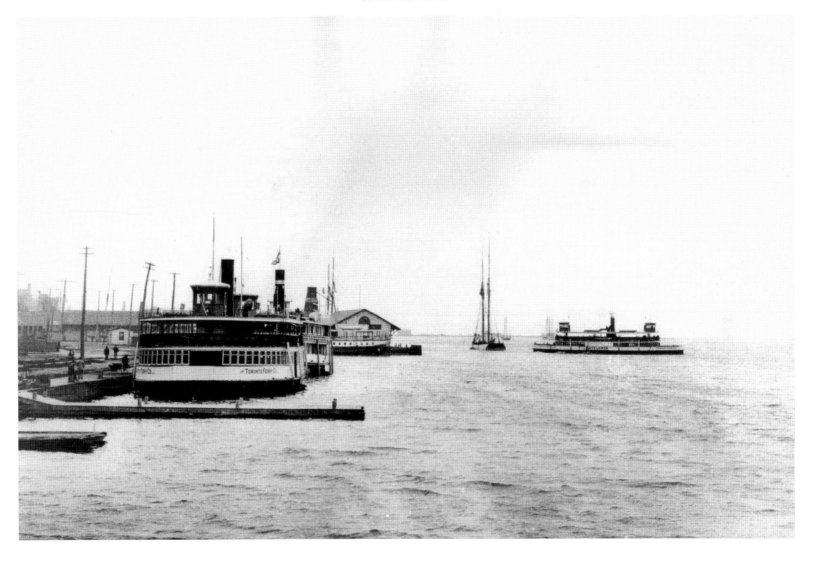

13 Steamers of the Toronto Ferry Company, 1898

The nearer paddle steamer and her sister ship in profile were the *Primrose* and the *Mayflower,* built at the foot of Bathurst Street in 1890. These vessels could each carry 900 passengers — the largest capacity of the island ferries of the time — and the company soon had a monopoly on all the island traffic. Both ships plied the bay until 1938 when, with the grievous mercilessness that seems to attend old age in ships, the sisters became freight scows, then scrapped.

The island must have been, as long as the wind did not come out of the north, a welcome relief from the smoky gloom and sooty air of the waterfront. The island also had positive attractions of its own: "the merry-go-round with its score or more of wooden horses and diminutive elephants, and its wheezy out-of-time organ, ... the 'great and only museum of living curiosities,' ... the fat lady from Central Africa, weighing 510 lbs, without her hairpins, ... a real live Zulu with an Irish accent, ... the switchback railway, the shooting galleries, the swings, the machines for testing your strength, and those for testing your nerves by electricity, ... an excellent band plays, and about once a week a little theatre is open for comic opera, the drama, burlesques, and what not ... terra cotta vases and other pieces of sculpture are dotted here and there ... Island Park will soon be second to none of the smaller parks around the city ... other cities regret that they have not such a spot."

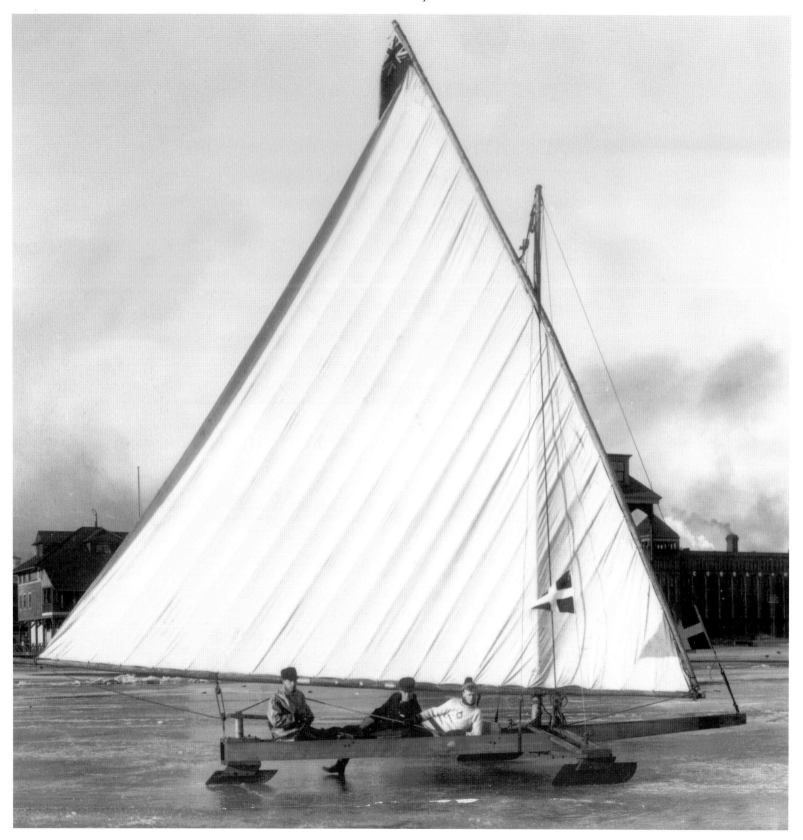

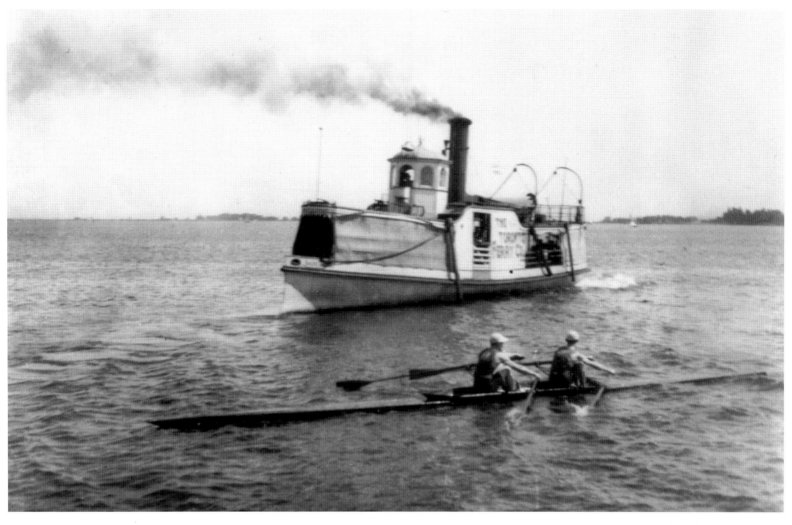

14 Iceboating on the harbour at the foot of York Street, c1900
15 The Luella

This tubby little steam ferry conveyed people to the island from 1880 to 1934. In her day she was considered "the handsomest boat in the bay and a great favourite with the island residents."

In the foreground (or forewater) is a scull, evoking a period in Toronto's sporting history when, instead of a motorbike or a car, a young man had a boat of some kind and belonged to one of the rowing clubs. There were races and regattas, camaraderie and competition, between the clubs and between other cities on the Lakes and in the northeastern States. World champion sculler Ned Hanlan was the hero of his day; once in England he was winning a race so easily that he pretended to collapse every so often, only to spring into action again as he was about to be overtaken.

But this merry fraternity was not beyond criticism from the city of churches on the mainland. "Nowadays a man who owns or rents a boathouse on the lake front is liable to have his motives questioned if such a thing as a camp bed is to be found, his friends usually eyeing each other quizzically. A pitiable story is told about the ruin of a young lady by one of the boathouse libertines. She was in the city during a convention and was induced to go for a row by her seducer, who landed at his own boathouse. She was a bewitching little beauty, and her betrayer was heard to boast of his dastardly act after she had left the city."

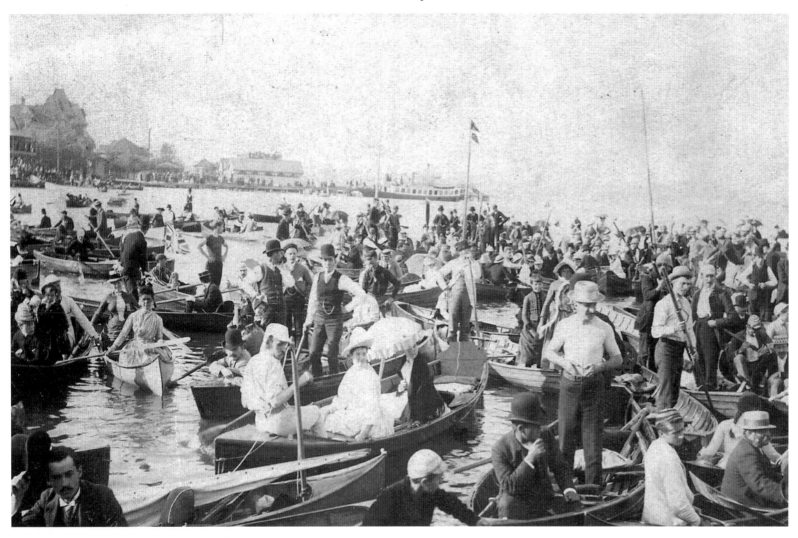

16 Spectators at a regatta off the Island, 1888

The water in the harbour was badly polluted long before 1888. The city's sewage ran untreated into the slips between the wharves. The water supply was drawn from the bay by pipes until 1873, when the city took over the utility and an intake tunnel was built out into the lake. Deaths from typhoid continued and were still common by 1888; people bought drinking water from carts.

This did not prevent jollification upon the waters, or men and boys, at least, from swimming in it. The Victorian lady may have been inhibited from going into the water more by her sense of modesty — and also perhaps by the lack of modesty of the men and boys who often wore nothing. Police regulations eventually required everyone to be clad from neck to knee for swimming in a public place.

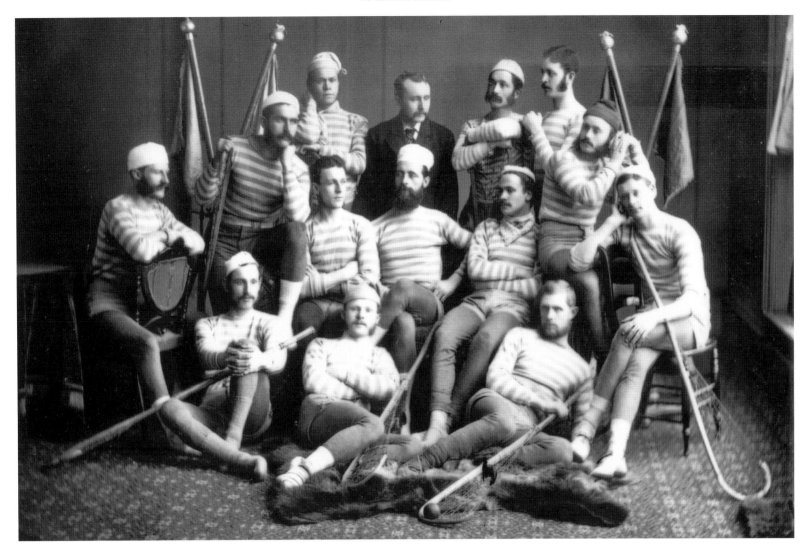

17 A Toronto Lacrosse team 1876

George Massey started the Toronto Lacrosse Club in 1867 and managed to build up quite a following. The club practised in Queen's Park and played matches on cricket grounds before purchasing grounds of its own in Rosedale. Its team was often world champion; its uniform was originally a "knicker-bocker costume with white cap." In 1867, it was argued that lacrosse should be Canada's national game; "Just as we declare the rivers, lakes and lands once Indian-owned to be now Canadian, so we claim the Indian field-game to be the national field-game of this Dominion.... Lacrosse, if favoured by good management and not made exclusive or seasoned with snobbishness as cricket often is, will find it heartily entered into by all classes of citizens." Sport was much more a matter of the many being observed by the few than the commercialized entertainment it has become today.

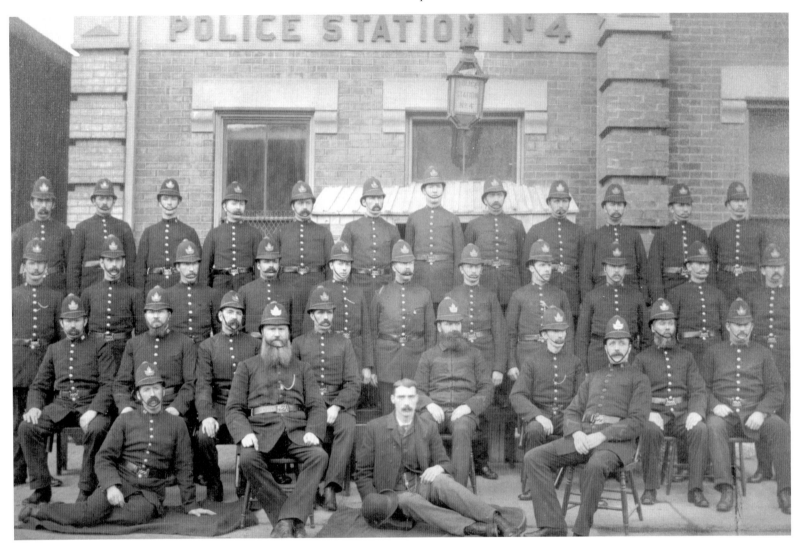

18 Members of the Toronto Police #4 Division (Dundas and Parliament Streets) 1884

In those days, policemen grew beards, which were not supposed to hide the number on the collar of their uniform. One of their main duties appears to have been to keep a sober enforcing eye on the drinking habits of Torontonians, though the Police Commissioners had to reprimand some of their own men at times for "intoxication" and "being found coming out of a brewery while on duty." The Island had a bad reputation for drunkenness and bootlegging on Sundays, when all proper Torontonians attended church, walked, talked, sang, read, and enjoyed themselves without unnecessary exuberance. Others had not the self-discipline or the attributes of bourgeois respectability to live so much for society and tomorrow, and a drinking spree was no doubt the quickest release from the stresses of wage slavery; in 1880, for instance, stablemen were working seven days a week, twelve hours a day, for $5. Manifold temperance organizations arose to combat the "social evil" of family suffering caused by overdrinking husbands. Some quacks claimed to be able to stop a craving not only for drink but also for drugs (morphine, cocaine, and opium).

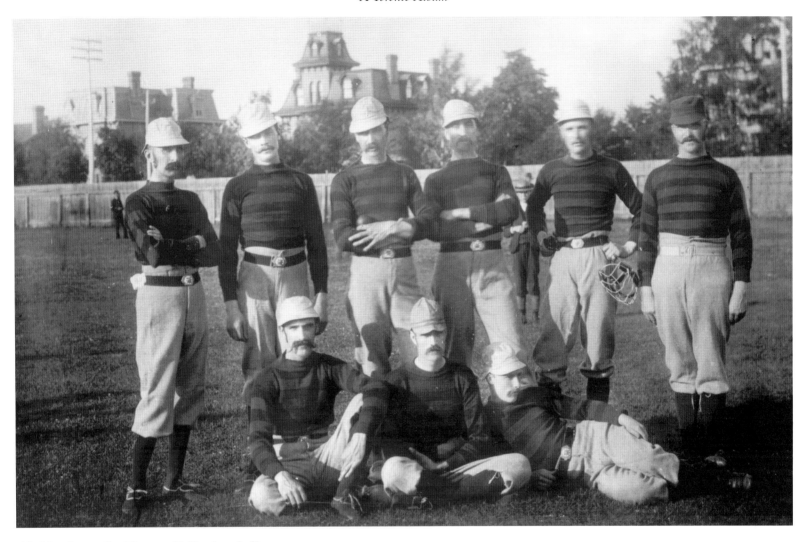

19 Members of a Toronto Police baseball team

In 1883, the Toronto Police Force Amateur Athletic Association was formed, and they joined in the energetic sporting activities of the city. There were horse races, with the riders standing on the backs of the galloping horses; bicycle races too, but cycling came to be enjoyed by people who might have been somewhat deterred by the rowdy enthusiasm common at competitive events. Among them might be the 20,000 delegates to the Third International Epworth League Convention (of Methodists) to whom this advice was offered in 1897:

"One of the most popular 'spins' is to take College Street west into High Park ... There is a cinder path for about four miles along the Lake Shore to the western terminus of Queen Street. Bicyclists in High Park should beware of coasting or even riding down the hills. They are tempting, but dangerous, and those who wish to preserve life and limb will do well to walk down.

"Arrangements have been completed to hold Sunrise Prayer Meetings for bicyclists on Friday and Saturday mornings. An early run will be made, starting from Headquarters Building at 5:30 a.m. The prayer meeting will be held at some point a few miles away, probably in High Park on Friday morning, and Reservoir Park on Saturday.

"Those who bring bicycles across the line will have to put up a deposit with the customs officers, which will be refunded on return. Wheels can be hired in Toronto at two hours for 25 cents in the day time and 35 cents in the evenings."

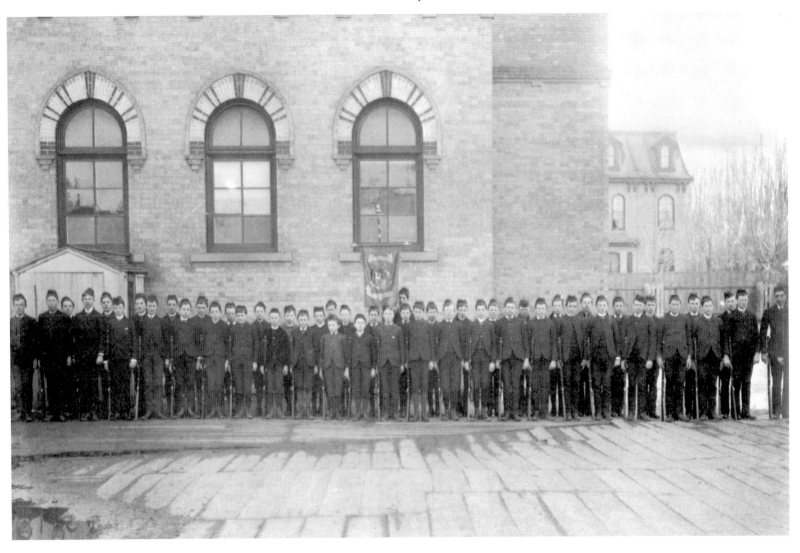

20 Boys of Wellesley Street school on parade, 1884

Toronto's (and Ontario's) public school system is legendarily attributed to "the work of one man of good sense and force of character": Egerton Ryerson. The provincial government sent him on tours of the United States, Britain, Ireland, and Europe, and Ryerson administered the system according to practices drawn from these various countries. The normal and model schools (for training teachers) imitated the Prussian system, and the original school texts were adapted from those used in the national schools in Ireland, where, in a triumph of compromise, books were created that satisfied both Protestants and Catholics. School attendance became compulsory in 1871, and in 1883, there were 15,250 children being taught by 1,993 teachers. Teachers' salaries were controversial, as always: male teachers earned on average $720 — and female teachers $324 — per year. There was overcrowding: "The teachers have not fair play in their endeavour to teach and discipline their classes." However, "the singing lesson ... is of no small hygienic use and does much to promote kindly feelings and the best sort of esprit de corps."

The Sutton Place Hotel now stands on the site of the school in this photograph.

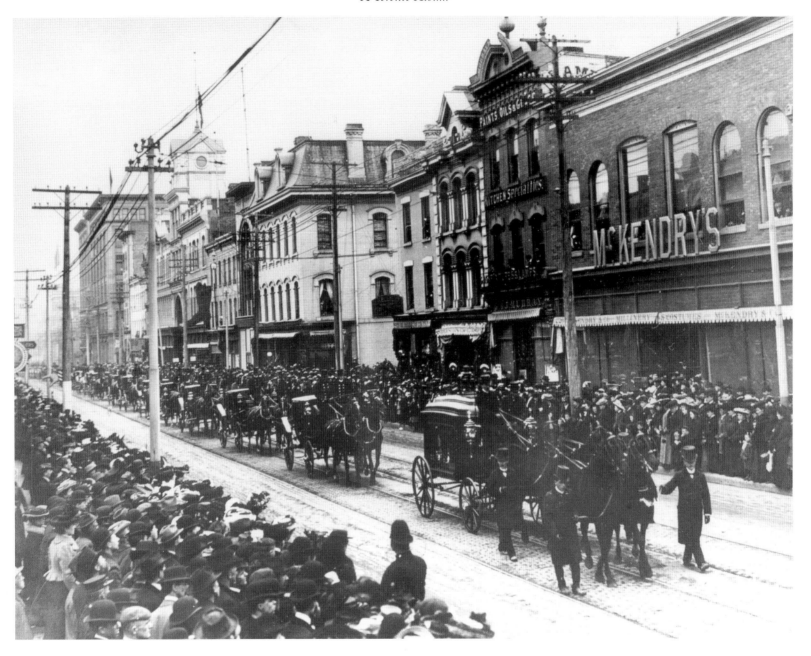

21 The funeral of Sir Oliver Mowat on Yonge Street north of Albert, April 22, 1903

Mowat, who was born in Kingston, Upper Canada, in 1820, was one of the province's most respected citizens. His monument in Mount Pleasant Cemetery lists some of his accomplishments: member of the Legislative Assembly of the Province of Canada, a "Father of Confederation," Premier of the Province of Ontario, Lieutenant Governor of Ontario, and a member of the Canadian Senate.

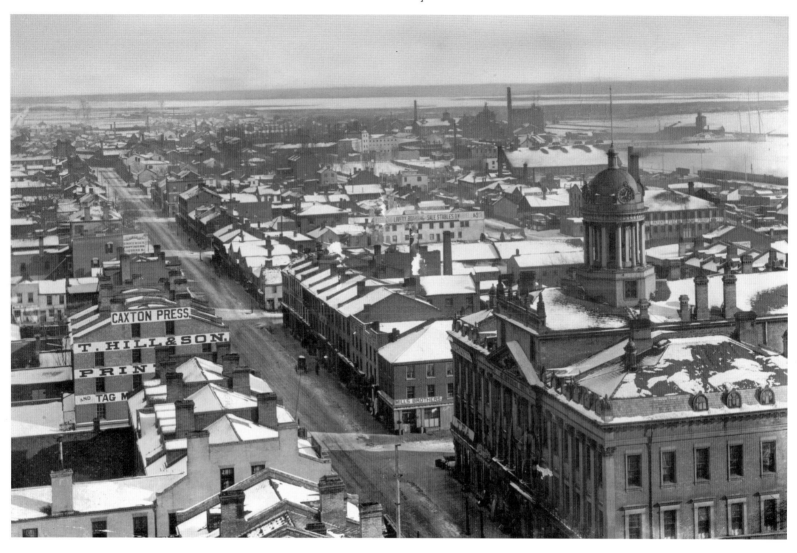

22 View from the tower of St. James' Cathedral, looking southeast

An earlier St. James', the primary Anglican Church of the city, was burned in the fire of 1849, and by 1853 the present cathedral was opened for use. The spire is 306 feet high and for a long time was the highest point in the city; the cathedral, unusually, faces south, so that the congregation faces north and not east — "the least ecclesiastical of all points of the compass, as it was in medieval times, reputed to be the residence of Satan himself."

In Canadian mythology, those of the north were "strong and free," and the Christmas fare offered in the St. Lawrence market across King Street bespoke a northern abundance — and appetite: "huge beef carcasses, rich with fat, hang side by side ... huge deer, the fat and greasy citizens of our forest, are suspended, picturesque with branching antlers ... black bear, in plump condition ere winter has thinned his fair proportions ... big pigs, and sucking pigs ... all manner of birds

of the air, the huge wild turkey, sometimes the rare wild swan, the prairie chicken, grouse and partridge."

The lettering "T. Hill and Son," as seen in the photo, on the west wall of the building at King and Jarvis, vanished when the building was beautifully restored by Stephen Callahan. It's now part of King George Square.

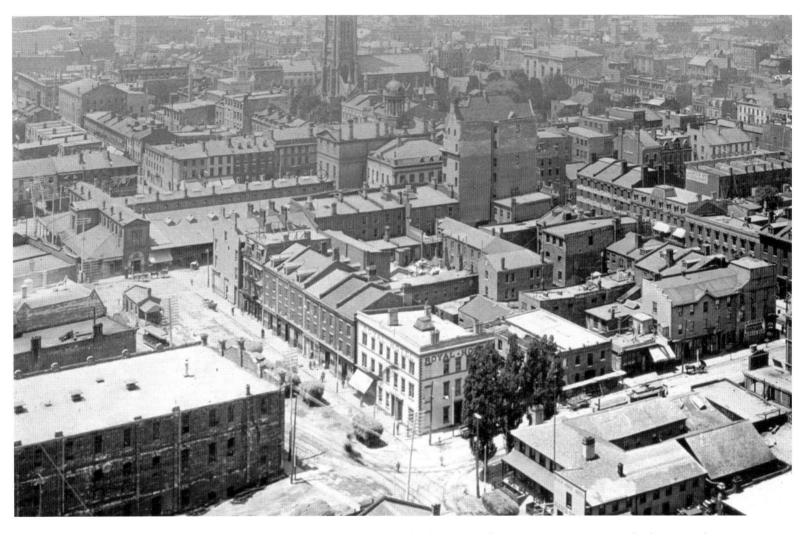

23 View from the chimney of the Toronto Railway Company at Sherbourne and Front streets in 1894, looking northwest

By 1883 Toronto had almost filled in the 5,400-acre site within the boundaries of the original 1834 city, and the next seven years saw a doubling of this area with the Town of Yorkville and then other areas — some built up like the "flowery suburb" of Parkdale and others not — systematically annexed. This expansion was accompanied by a great deal of land speculation and resulted in higher taxes. But the population continued to increase, and the new areas were soon, for the most part, the homes and gardens of the middle classes.

By 1890, the city limits reached in the west to High Park (an estate offered to the city in 1873 for an annuity of $1,200 by J.C. Howard on condition that it would be a "pleasure-ground" forever), then along the foot of the escarpment that was the natural northern boundary to the plain on which the city was built, responded to the northerly pull of Yonge Street, and across the Don to include land along Kingston Road.

The record of population growth in the city is as follows:

1834	9,000
1844	18,000
1854	38,000
1864	45,000
1874	68,000
1884	105,000
1894	168,000
1904	226,000
1924	542,000
1934	640,000

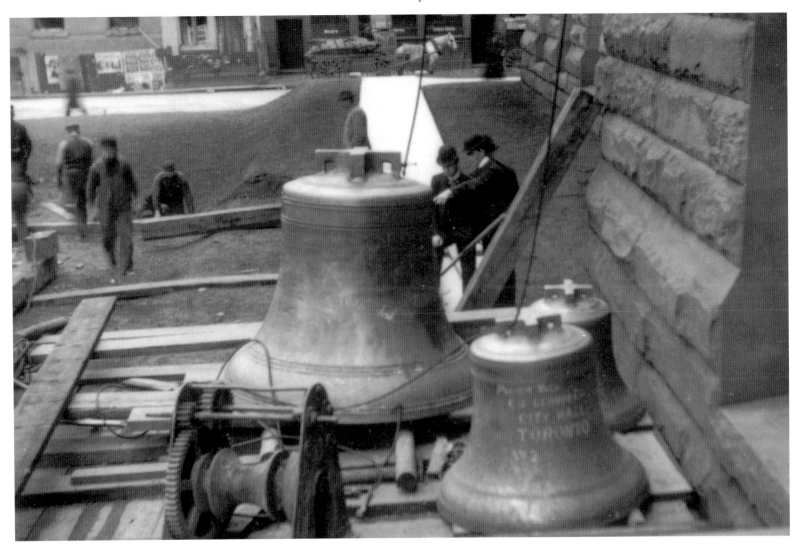

24 Bells for Toronto, 1899

In 1884, the city had expropriated a site at the head of Bay Street on Queen Street for a new courthouse, but in 1887 it decided to combine the courthouse with a new administrative centre for the city. E.J. Lennox from Toronto won the design competition, and in 1899 City Hall was opened. It had, of course, cost far more than had been budgeted; but one mayor thought that the presence of such a monument symbolized that "the mental and moral natures" of Torontonians were now "above the faculties of the beasts." Others thought that the money would have been better spent on sanitary improvements. Built of red sandstone from near the forks of Credit, stone that was used in building many of the houses on the university's lots along St. George Street, it remains an impressive example of the North American Romanesque style. The three bells for Toronto's "Big Ben" weigh: hour bell — 11,648 lbs.; half-hour bell — 3,339 lbs.; and quarter-hour bell — 1,904 lbs. They were in place in time to ring in the twentieth century when the year 1900 advanced to 1901.

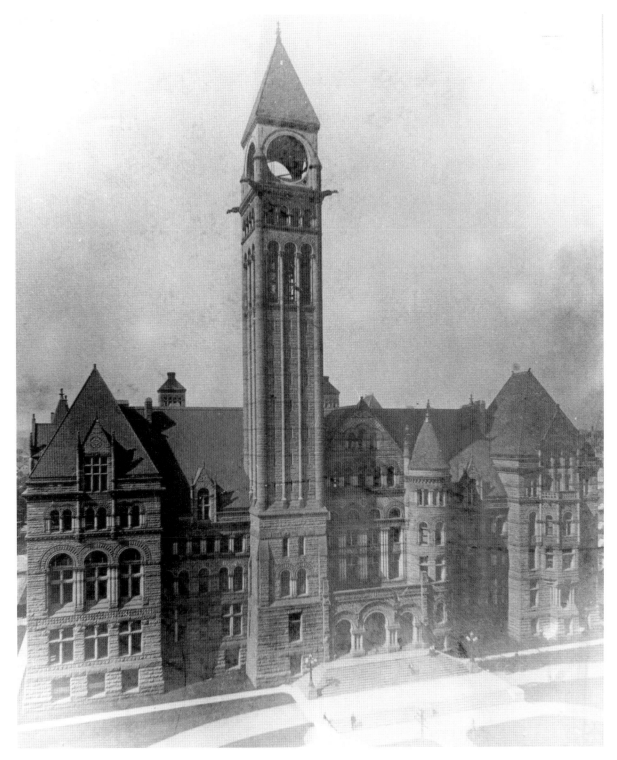

25 The new City Hall without its clock

26 Looking north on Yonge Street from south of Adelaide, June 1900

The sour relations between British and Boer Settlers in South Africa led to war in the fall of 1899. Much of English-speaking Canada responded to this challenge to the Empire with what later seemed a "jingoistic outburst" of enthusiasm. Toronto's loyalty to the Crown and Empire was indeed a "passion" at the time. In the simple verse of Alexander Muir: "The month it was October, The year was ninety-nine, When Johnny Canuck first left his house To join the British line."

The federal government sent two contingents of some 3,000 officers and men to fight the Boers. Toronto militia formed "C" Company of the first contingent; "cheery crowds were in the armouries nightly," and the City Council gave to each officer $25 in cash and a field glass, and to each enlisted man $5 and a silver matchbox; it also insured the lives of each Toronto man who went off to the war for $1,000. The city's farewell to "C" Company was a scene of "almost delirious enthusiasm."

The fortunes of war at first favoured the Boers, but the tide of battle turned with the first engagement in which Canadians were involved — at Paardeberg in February 1900 — and within three months General Roberts had led his troops into the Boer capital of Pretoria. The occupation of Pretoria was assumed to mean that the war had been won, and a false report of its fall caused a premature outburst of jubilation in Toronto.

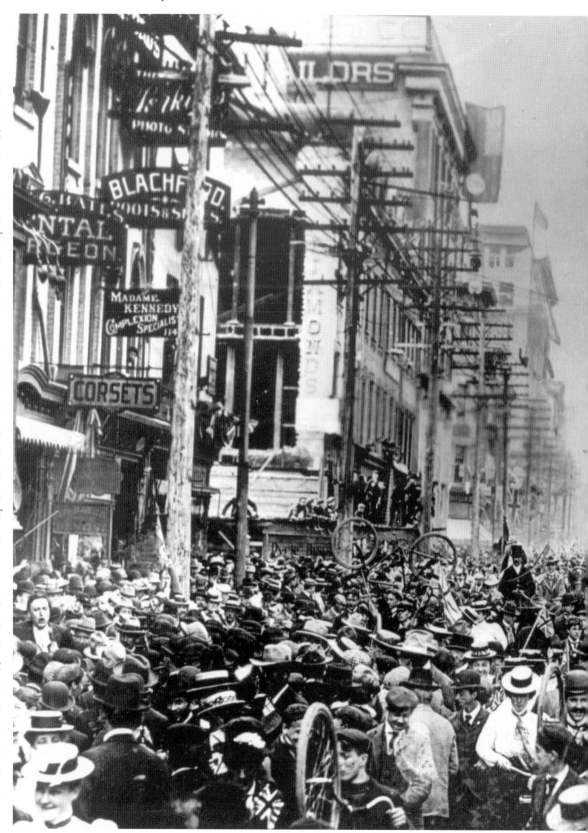

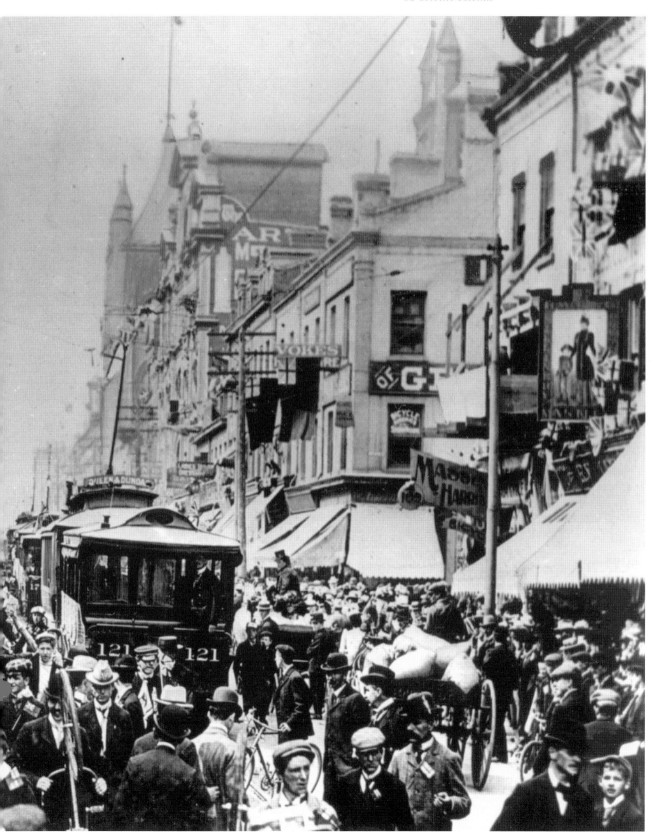

Several years after the war concluded, the South African War Memorial was erected on University Avenue, north of Queen, to honour all Canadians who lost their lives in the conflict. The impressive structure had to be moved from its original location to accomodate the construction of the University subway.

27 Looking south on University Avenue at College, October 1901

The South African War was not over, however; the Canadian troops returned quickly, but fighting dragged on for two more years as the British tried to suppress the Boer commandos.

During this inglorious stage of the war, Queen Victoria died, and was succeeded by her son as Edward VII, who had made the first Royal Visit to Toronto in 1860 and whose equestrian statue is now the main sight to be seen in Queen's Park. The new king's son and his wife, the Duke and Duchess of Cornwall and York, were sent off at once on an Imperial cruise, arriving in Toronto in October 1901. Anxious to excel the city's 1860 welcome, a group of Toronto manufacturers raised $10,000 to build this triumphal arch in stucco. The Independent Order of Foresters built one no less elaborate at the corner of Bay and Richmond streets. "Electric lights were used with great freedom by all the merchants and the business section of the city was gay with flags and bunting."

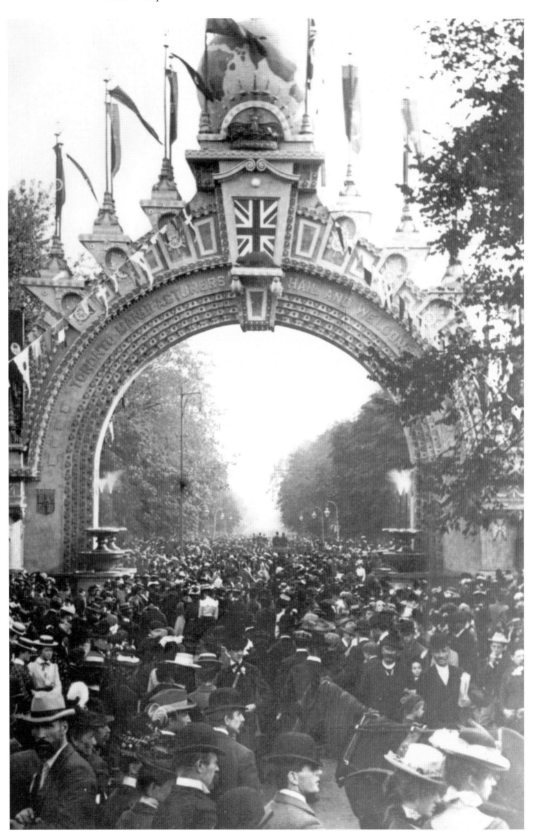

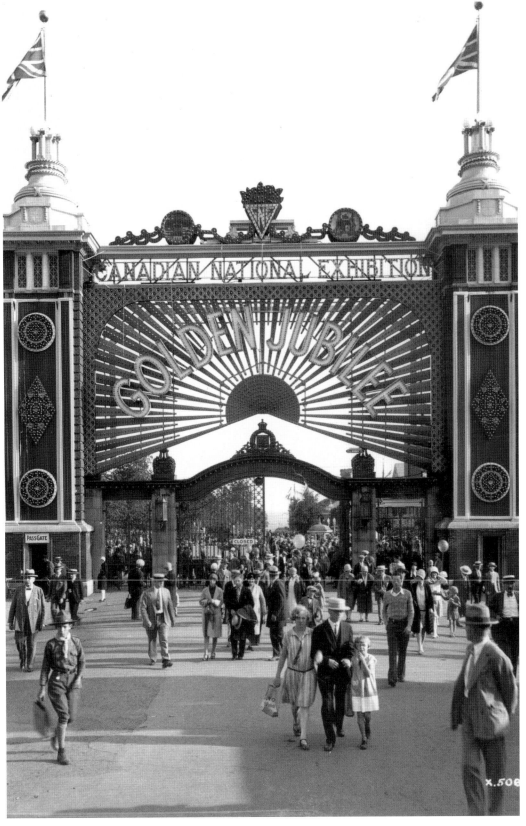

28 The Dufferin Gate, Exhibition Park, 1928

Such flamboyant arches were usually temporary, and were once termed "civic signs of joy." One was built for the soldiers when they came home from the South African war, but the Dufferin Gate was intended to be more permanent. It was built in 1912 and is shown here specially bedecked for the fiftieth anniversary of the founding of the Industrial Exhibition Association of Toronto. Exhibitions had been held previously: in 1858 Toronto's own Crystal Palace had been erected — seven years after the larger London one and two years before Montreal's — on land by the lake that had been part of the military reserve. Thus had begun, in imitative splendour, what was to develop into one of Toronto's greatest social institutions, bringing families from the surrounding countryside for an annual harvest-time and pre-school celebration in the capital. Until after the Second World War the price of admission was a quarter. It wasn't until 1912 that the Toronto Industrial Exhibition became more popularly known as the Canadian National Exhibition; in 1928 attendance broke two million for the first time.

The first commercial electric passenger railway in the world operated in Toronto in 1884. It ran from Strachan Avenue into the Exhibition Grounds "making a good deal of noise and shooting sparks."

The gate in the photo was demolished to make way for the new Gardiner Expressway. The present Dufferin Gate was erected in 1959.

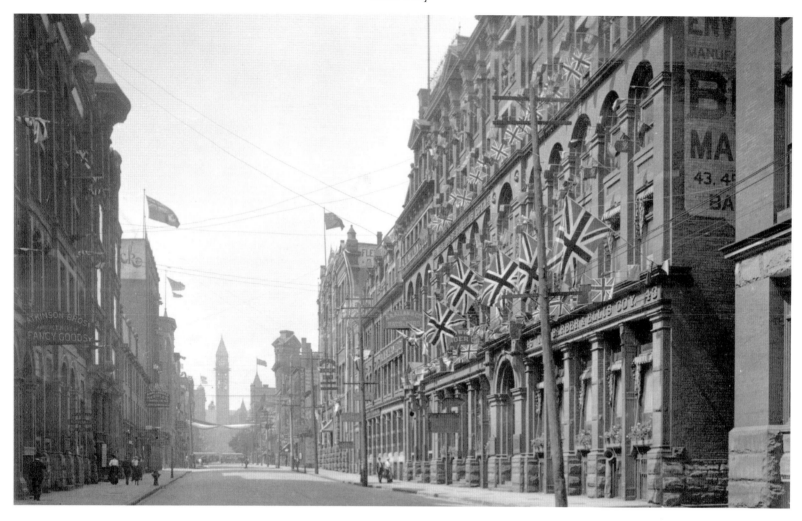

29 Bay Street looking north to the new City Hall, c1902

Bay Street was not yet a canyon of financial
offices and the British influence is evidenced
by the many business offices bedecked with
Union jacks and red, white, and blue bunting.

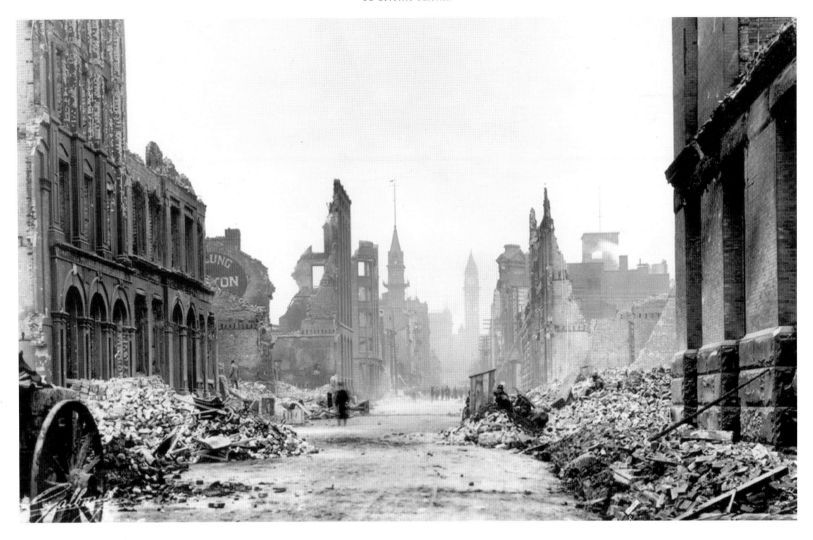

30 Bay Street after the fire of 1904

Toronto's most disastrous fire broke out in the E. and S. Currie neckwear factory on the north side of Wellington just off Bay Street on the evening of April 19, 1904. It was attributed to a defect in the electrical wiring and was discovered about 8 p.m. The evening was windy and by the morning fourteen acres had been razed. In total, 86 buildings were destroyed, affecting 137 businesses and inflicting nearly $13 million in damages. More than 5,000 people were out of work. Gordon Mackay and Co., W.G. Gage, Warwick Brothers and Rutter, Brown Brothers and Copp Clark were among the long-established companies whose offices and stock were destroyed. Firemen came from as far away as Hamilton, Niagara Falls, Buffalo, Peterborough, Brantford, and London; by train, with their equipment on flat cars to offer assistance. But the pressure in the city hydrants was very low and by midnight the area south of Bay and Melinda, east to Front and Yonge, and west to the Queen's Hotel was a seething furnace. Staff and guests in the popular Queen's Hotel patrolled the roof to extinguish any burning material carried by the wind and put wet blankets against the window frames, and so saved the building. As the *Star* newspaper subsequently reported the conflagration, "the fire ate millions in property, but no one was killed." Valuable documents held in company safes usually survived, but the managers of one business opened their safe too soon, only to see the documents ignite before their eyes.

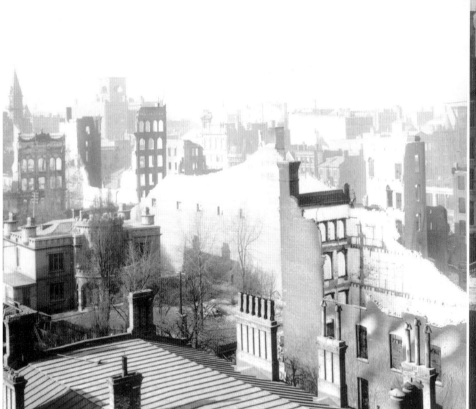
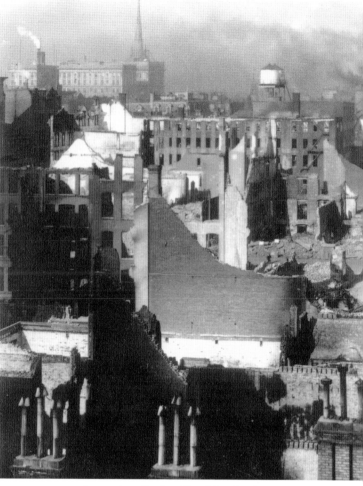

31 Looking from the Queen's Hotel east along Front Street after the fire

The following account of the fire was told by a streetcar motorman to his son who recorded the details:

> My dad was running a relief (street)car on Yonge Street and was southbound on Yonge when the first fire reels went west on Wellington. Dad went along Front, around Station loop and on reaching Wellington Street he and his conductor looked along that street. What looked like a very ordinary fire was being fought west of Bay Street.

There was a lot of smoke, and firemen with lanterns could be seen running around, but it did not look serious. Continuing north on Yonge, more fire rigs were met, rushing south on Yonge. Then as their car was passing Fire Hall No 3 at Yonge and Grosvenor, they heard the "general alarm" ringing from the tower.

When Dad wyed at Price Street to return south, he could see an angry red glow in the sky, but still could not credit the Wellington fire for such a display. On this trip downtown, he carried a heavy load of sightseers, hurrying down to watch the fire. When they reached Wellington Street, they found that the fire had jumped that street and several buildings on its south side were in flames. Proceeding south a block, then west on Front Street, they were held up momentarily by steam fire engines coupling up to hydrants on Front Street. Firemen were frantically trying to find a hydrant with a good supply of water, and the engines were being moved around

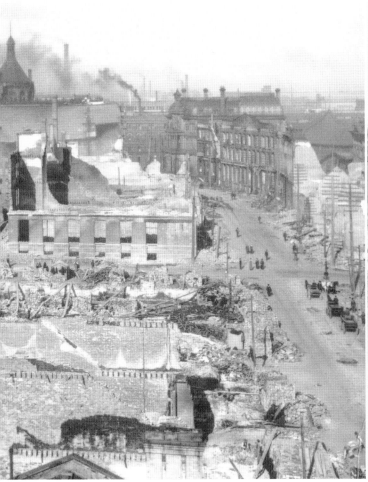
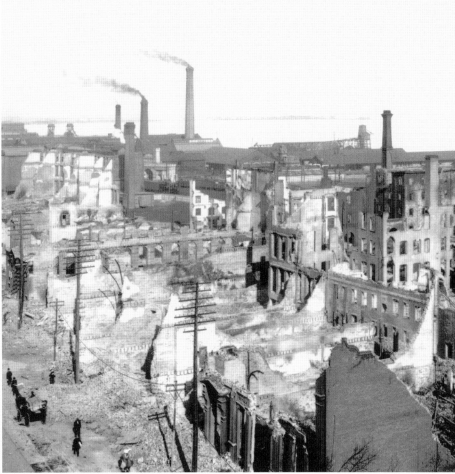

repeatedly. Dad went around Station loop and back east on Front as hose was being strung across the street.

All southbound cars were now carrying capacity loads of citizens heading for the greatest fire in the city's history. Front Street west of Bay was completely blocked off ... When Dad's car arrived southbound at Wellington, the power went off for a few seconds; as he approached Front the power was cut off and remained off for two days.

Dad and his conductor took turns at watching the fire and look-

ing after their car. The fire was heading in their direction and about midnight firemen appeared on Yonge Street, running their hose lines into the buildings on the west side of Yonge. Dad's conductor went to the nearest saloon for a bucket of beer and the barkeep sent along a bottle of 'something to keep the fire boys warm.' Every few minutes a fireman or a policeman would board the darkened streetcar to emerge a few moments later wiping his mouth.

Firemen from Buffalo, NY, arrived and started drawing water

from the bay; their fine efforts saved the Customs House at the southwest corner of Yonge and Front. Towards dawn, Dad and his conductor were forced to leave their car when the fire reached Yonge Street, burning out the building where their car was standing. This was the only point on Yonge touched by the fire. Shortly after eight o'clock in the morning, power was turned on long enough to back the car to safety. The weather was cold, ice had formed on the tracks, and Dad was forced to use his switch iron in order to free the car.

32 Toronto Firehalls

Firehall No. 12, at the northwest corner of Bolton and Allen, built 1884.

Firehall No. 10, on the north side of Yorkville Avenue, built 1876.

Firehall No. 11, at the southwest corner of Rose and Howard, built in 1884.

Firehall No. 7, on Wilton Avenue (now Dundas Street) west of Parliament, built 1878.

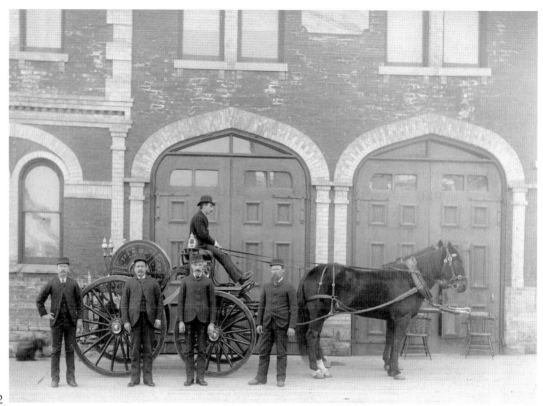

Firehall No. 12

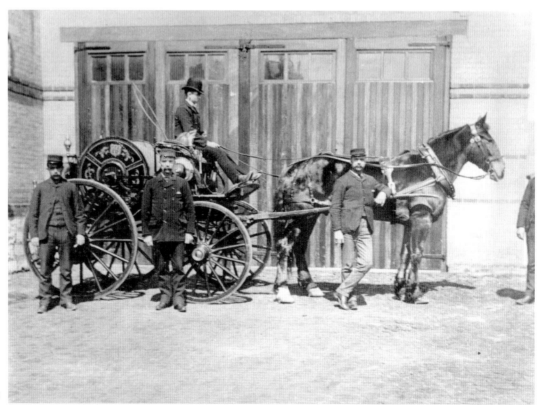

Firehall No. 10

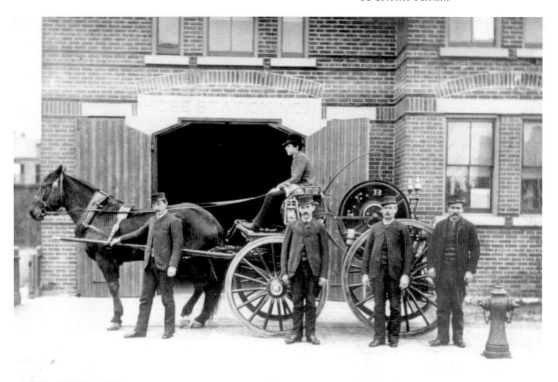

Firehall No. 11

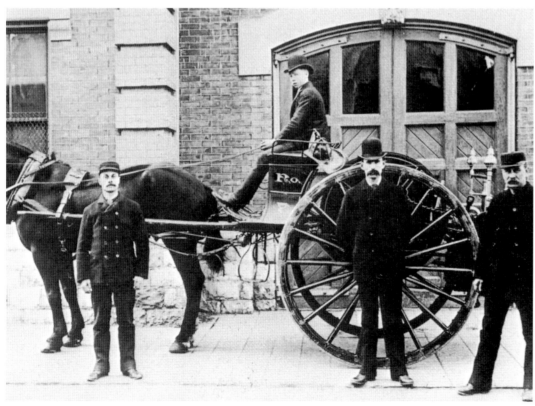

Firehall No. 7

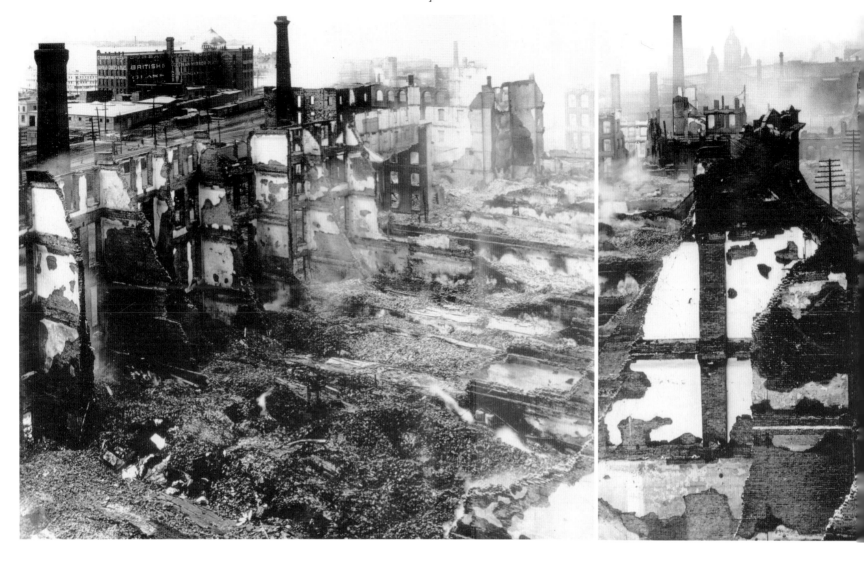

*33 Looking west along Front Street from the
Customs House at the corner of Yonge after the fire*

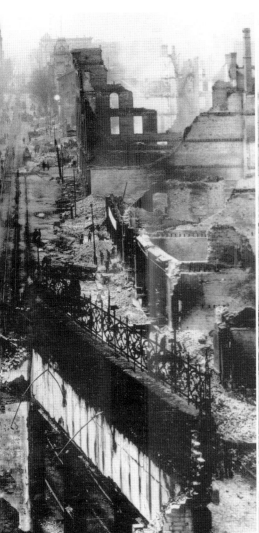
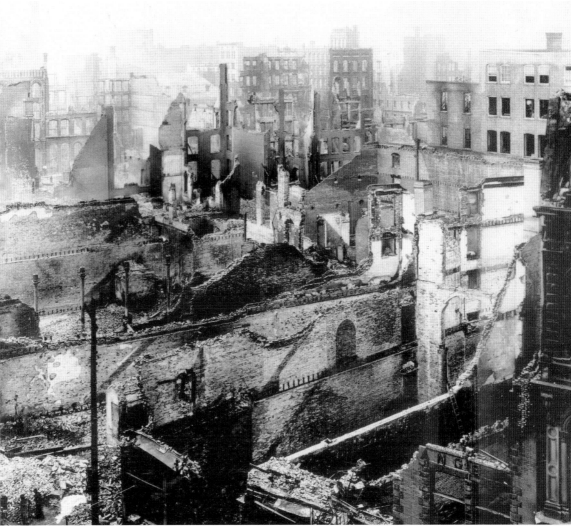

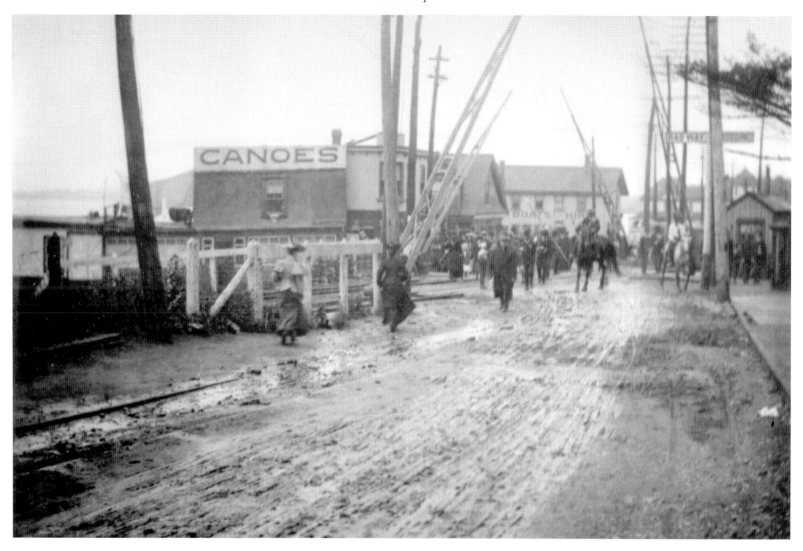

34 Sunnyside Crossing in the early 1900s

At this time, Queen Street West crossed the lines of the Grand Trunk Railway at grade where it became the Lakeshore Road. It continued, south of the tracks, in a westerly direction across the Humber. A hotel on Lakeshore Road at the Humber River can be seen in the background. The Queen streetcar line stopped before the rail crossing and passengers walked over the tracks to catch one of the double-deck cars that ran for a few years out to suburban Mimico.

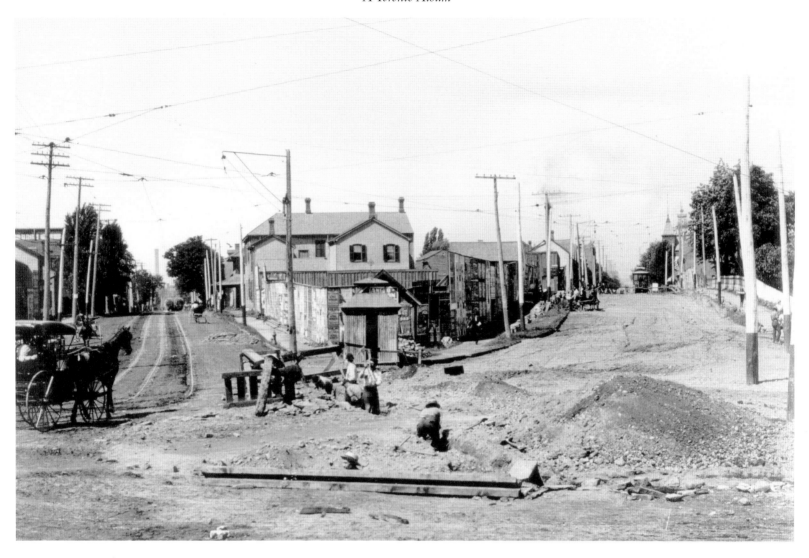

35 The junction of King and Queen streets at the Don River in 1900

A strangely Siberian scene; in 1897, the King cars ran as far east as Munro Park, where the local residents, unwilling to have a streetcar service of any kind, tore up new-laid rails and dumped them in the ditch. The old Don station (recently moved to Todmorden Mills Park) would be to the left of the view. The streetcar and train tracks crossed each other at grade until a new bridge was built over the railway and the river a few years before the First World War.

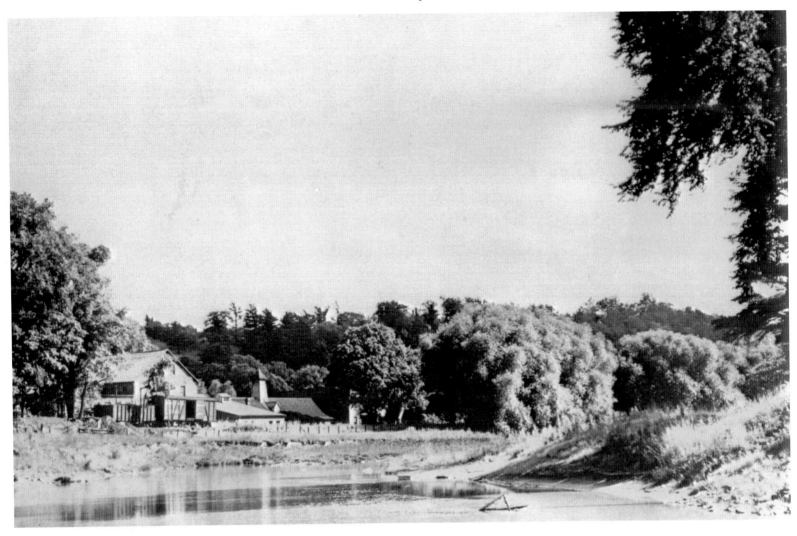

36 A paper mill in the Don Valley, c1900

No matter how unattractive the city may have been, where it reached the watercourses that formed its early topographical boundaries, one could find the natural beauties of the rivers and their banks. The Don River had been used to drive mills at various locations along its length for almost a hundred years. The salmon and trout had long since disappeared from its no longer pure waters, and downstream it was a notorious sewer. At present, only one paper mill remains of the three that John Taylor and his two brothers built, the first one to supply paper for the *Globe* newspaper as early as 1845. The upper mill was at the forks of the east and west branches of the Don down to which the Don Mills road ran from Todmorden; the middle mill, enlarged, was still in operation in 1970; and the lower mill, on the site of the East York's Todmorden Mills Park, burned down in 1900. These mills were small enough, however, not to dominate the Sylvan Valley or, apart from their effect on the water, to upset the ecology. They made paper from rags and other related products, including something called "Taylor's Mothproof Carpet Paper." It was made from cedar bark, much of which came from the yards where the city paving blocks were prepared. In summer the supply of bark occasionally ran out and a man was sent out with a scythe to cut down neighbouring thistles as a partial substitute.

Today, there are no operational mills on the lower Don River.

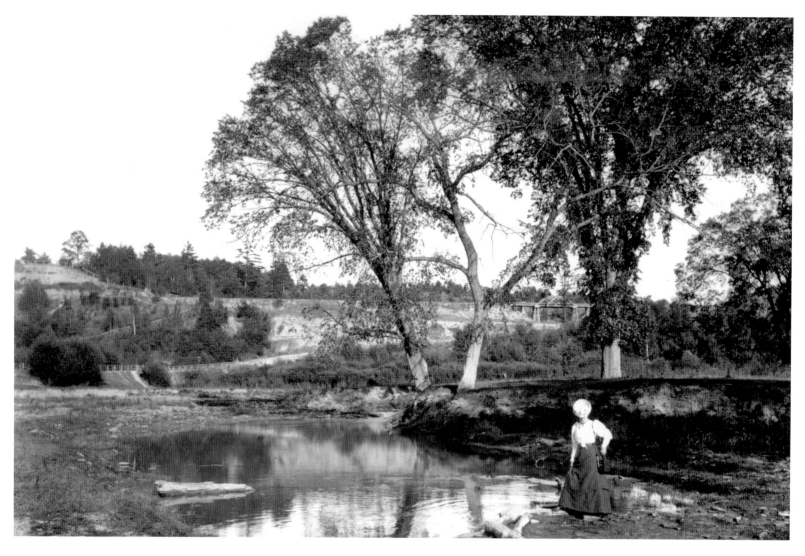

37 *An idyll on the Humber*

In the background is a railway bridge on the "Humber Loop" of the old Belt Line Railway, an unsuccessful comuter line that ran parallel to the river near Bloor Street.

The charms of the Humber were celebrated in the Toronto Railway Company's Tourist Booklet for 1894. "There is no lack of lovely places in and around Toronto, but few to equal the beauties in the neighborhood of Humber Bay. A panorama of glorious views greets the passenger along this route ... passing through one of the brightest stretches of landscape on the face of the earth. Passengers can leave the cars anywhere along the route to gambol on the beach or to meander through the wooded nooks along the line ... the trolley tourist can take a row up the charming river or a sail on the lake, away from the turmoil and danger of the steamers ... A short distance further west is another little river, too small for boating, but just the thing for bathing; it has a fine sandy bottom and is deep enough for a swim without fear of drowning ... There are cars to and fro every twenty minutes, and the fare is five cents, or six tickets for a quarter."

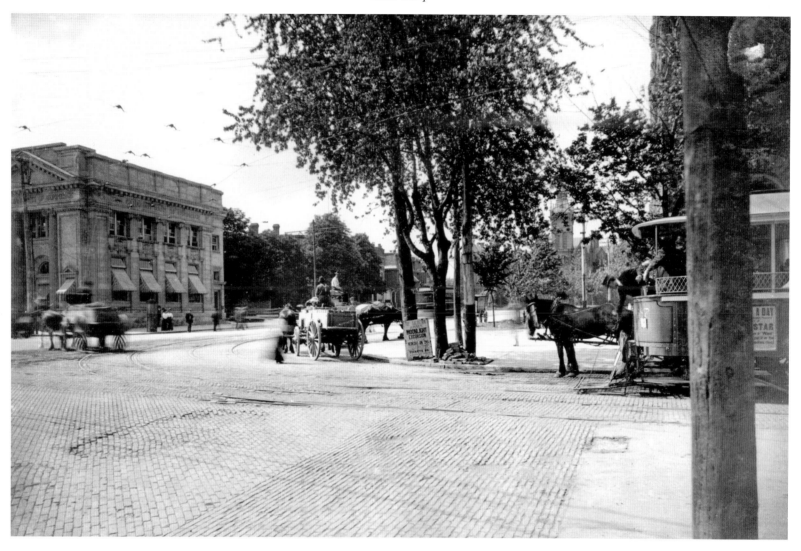

38 Looking north on Spadina from College, c1900

In 1861, the Toronto Street Railway Company had received a thirty-year franchise to run their horse-drawn vehicles through the city. By the end of their franchise, their inventory included 262 streetcars, 99 omnibuses, 100 sleighs, and 1,372 horses, all of which were kept in stables located at Front and George, Front and Frederick, King Street near the Don, and on Yorkville Avenue. They had laid some sixty-eight miles of track before the city bought them out and ran the system itself for a few months.

In 1891, a new company, the Toronto Railway Company, was formed on the initiative of William Mackenzie to acquire the franchise for another thirty years. This company proceeded to electrify the system it had bought, adding their overhead wires to the existing tangle of lines along the streets. The first electrically powered TRC car ran on Church Street on August 15, 1892; the last horse car trotted down McCaul Street on August 31, 1894. For a time, the TRC was full of enthusiasm for improving the system and promoting its usefulness *(see the quotation with photograph 42)*.

Religious pressures precluded the city streetcars from running on Sundays until May 23, 1897.

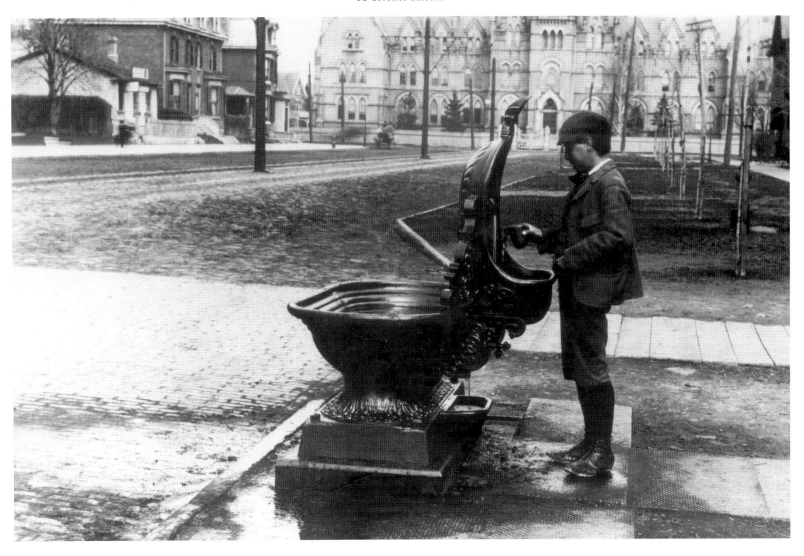

39 Horse trough on the east side of Spadina at College, 1899

Spadina Avenue, which was laid out by the ubiquitous Dr. W.W. Baldwin, was acquired by the city in the 1840s. Originally, the thoroughfare was constructed as an approach to the doctor's country house on the escarpment near the present Casa Loma. No doubt envisagening a noble boulevard, perhaps like the Paris, France's noble Champs Elysees, it was laid out to the munificent width of 160 feet, twice that of Toronto's main streets. Along part of its length were trees lining the sidewalks as well as two rows of trees bracketing a streetcar boulevard in the centre. The first few buildings, in place by the 1880s, were described as "sumptuous mansions chiefly of the new Queen Anne style." Later buildings were not of great architectural worth except for Knox College, which was erected in the circle above College Street in 1875. Here, ministers were trained in the Presbyterian faith. During the Great War the building was a military hospital and later served as an insulin factory. Today, challenged by the mass horsepower of automobiles, the lovely old building seems very fragile.

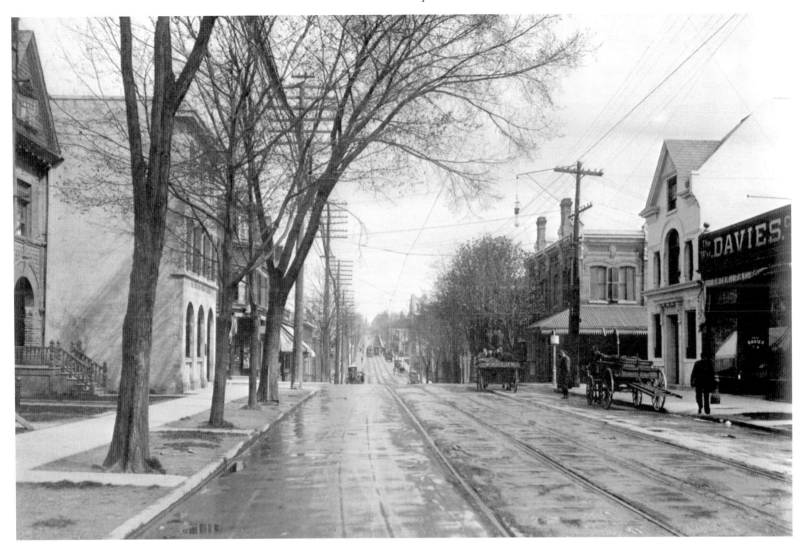

40 *Looking north on Avenue Road from below Davenport Road, 1907*

In the far distance can be seen the spire of Upper Canada College. The CP railway tracks crossed the street at grade until 1912 when a series of subways (now described as underpasses) were built from Yonge to Ossington. In 1903, a "stub" streetcar track was laid along Dupont Street running west to between Walmer and Kendal avenues. One small streetcar rocked along this track and it was known by the locals as the "Cannonball Express," ironically so, for the motorman came to know the residents and always waited for anyone wishing a ride. On the right is Wm. Davies' store — an enterprise that profited greatly from supplying meat to the Canadian troops in the First World War. It eventually became part of the newly established Canada Packers. Hanging above the store is an electric arc lamp. A rope and pulley affair allowed the lamp to be lowered every day so the carbon rods could be trimmed. When they were first installed in the 1880s people would crowd around and watch them sputter and fizzle. This service was in the hands of the Toronto Electric Light Company, another enterprise of William Mackenzie, who charged 62 cents per lamp per night; the company was very profitable.

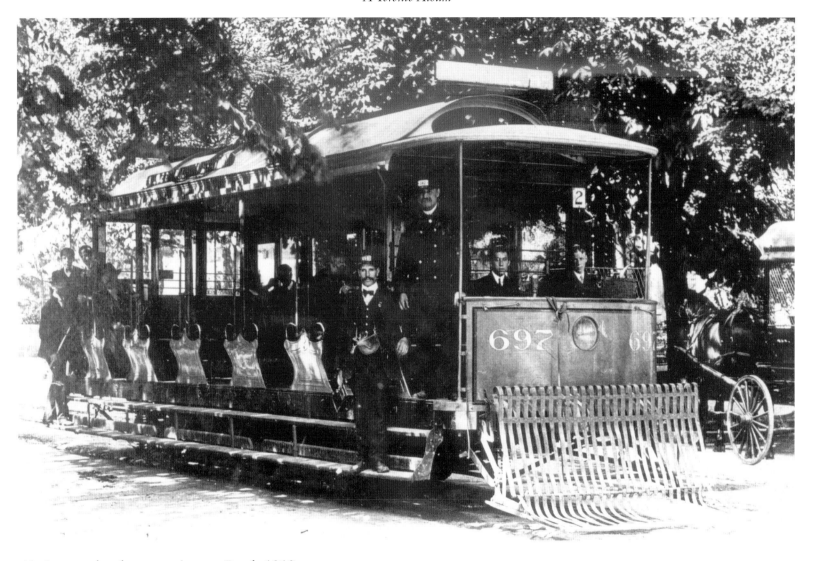

41 An open-bench car on Avenue Road, 1910

These single-truck cars were of the "convertible" variety, meaning that in the winter sides and windows, that had been removed for the summer season, could be re-installed as was a coal-burning stove. Electric heating of the cars, while available, was found to be too costly and somehow endangered passengers, as was proven when a newspaper stuck behind one of the stoves caused a disastrous fire in the King Street barns in 1916.

In summer, it must have been delightful to travel in such a breezy way along the tree-shaded streets, with the conductor swinging along the side-steps collecting fares. In the evening, the streetcars carried one or two coloured lights under the route sign as a means of route identification. Cars on the Avenue Road line showed two white lights, while one white light identified a King car, and the Belt Line was known by its single red light. In the summer, parties rented the streetcars for private "moonlight excursions," each car "being specially fitted up with cluster and festooned electric lamps, and they travel in a blaze of incandescent glory wherever they go."

42 TRC Belt Line car on Spadina at College, 1919

The TRC's "Belt Line" (not to be confused with the steam engine Belt Line described later) ran both directions on Spadina, King, and Sherbourne, and on tracks laid in 1889 on Bloor. The company described the route thus:

A better general idea can be obtained of Toronto by a ride round the Belt Line than in any other way. It encircles the major part of the city, the splendid retail stores of King Street, the handsome residences of the merchant princes in the suburbs, as well as a part of the older and less wealth locality, passing in review on this favourite route. Half way up Sherbourne Street is the Horticultural Gardens. At Bloor Street the cars turn westward past scores of the finest private mansions in Canada. Most of the great educational institutes, for which Toronto is justly famous, are on the Belt Line, and it passes all the leading hotels, and crosses all the other streetcar routes. The Belt Line trip is one of the most popular and interesting of the entire system, and during the summer evenings the cars on this line are crowded with ladies and babies out for an airing, and physicians prescribe this trip very generally as a most refreshing bedtime stimulant and diversion.

Other potential uses of the streetcar are described in the accompanying extract from a TRC brochure:

The trolley postal car, designed to

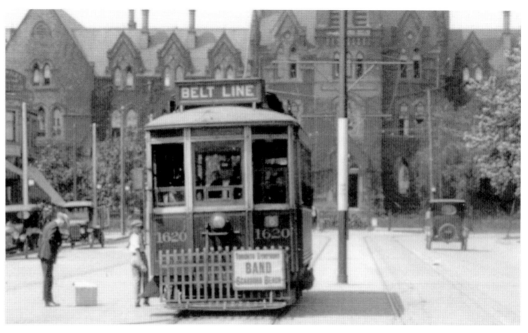

facilitate the collections and distribution of mail matter is now being tested in one or two leading cities in the United States. As soon as its practical utility has been firmly established, the Toronto Railway Company will be ready to adopt the idea on the recommendation of the postal authorities.

In time there may be a demand for a local and suburban express and freight service by trolley cars. When that time arrives the company will be ready to operate a special service for that purpose.

A partial test was made of conveying the city's garbage in trolley carts by night. In time, the company, ever ready to extend its usefulness, may be asked to supply this service under a permanent arrangement.

Other bright suggestions come from clever people, and all receive careful attention. Usually however,

they are unique rather than useful.

For instance, one idea recently suggested by a Toronto undertaker, proposed the operation of a specially constructed private funeral car. His design represented a long car, finished in black, trimmed in silver and hung with black curtains. The forward quarter section of the car was to be enclosed and provided for the reception of the casket, and the remainder of the car, furnished in sumptuous but sombre upholstering, for the mourners. The suggestion bristled with details but — at present the company is wholly engaged in continually improving the service for live people.

Streetcars returned to Spadina Avenue with the opening of the Spadina LRT line on July 27, 1997.

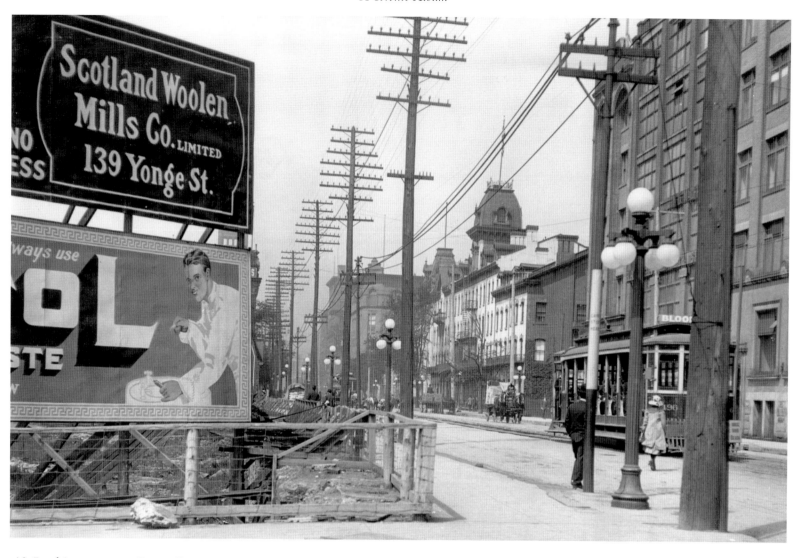

43 Looking west on Front Street, 1916

In the background is Queen's Hotel, and to the left is an area burned over by the 1904 fire where construction of the present Union Station had already begun. The clustered electric lights might remind some Torontonians of the war being waged between, on one side, the city and the Ontario Hydro-Electric Power Commission, and on the other, Sir William Mackenzie (he had been knighted in 1911) and his Toronto Electric Light Company (TELCO). The contest began with a concern among many southern Ontario municipalities that the hydro-electric power about to be generated at Niagara might all flow to the United States. Here in Toronto members of City Council decided that the city should purchase and distribute this new (and much cheaper) energy itself. Niagara power reached Toronto in 1911, by which time Toronto Hydro had completed a distribution system of its own in direct competition with that of TELCO. In 1920, the Mackenzie hydro properties, including a mammoth generating plant at Niagara Falls, Ontario, were bought up by Ontario Hydro and its allied municipalities.

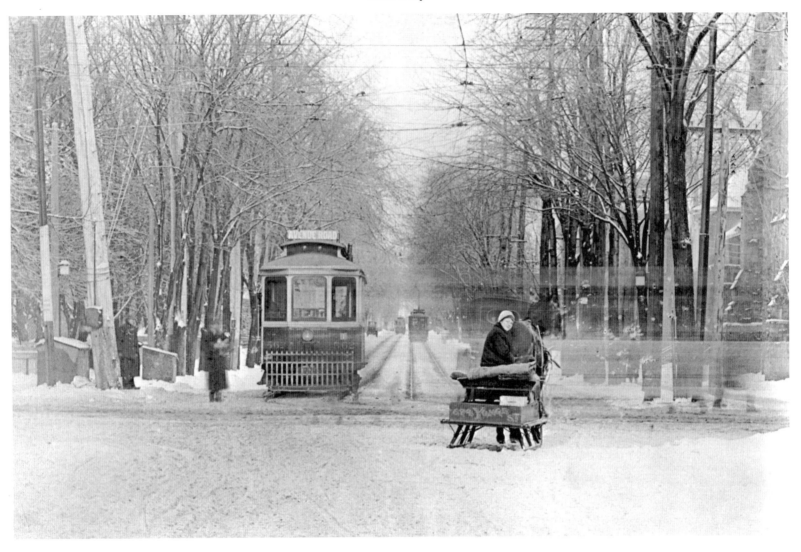

44 *Looking north on Avenue Road from Bloor Street, 1912*

Track had been laid from Bloor Street up Avenue Road in 1903, reached St. Clair by 1906. At one point city officials ordered police to stop the track gangs from working because it feared that Mackenzie was going to connect up with the other lines he owned and would move huge freight cars through the centre of the city. Judging by the overhead wires in this photo, the TRC must have anticiapted running its track south into Queen's Park. This was never permitted. For years, the entrance to Queen's Park was adorned with two orna-mental gateposts, presented to the city by the Imperial Order of the Daughters of the Empire in honour of the Royal visit of 1901. Subsequently, the gates were moved to a new location at the Bloor Street end of "Philosophers Walk" that winds through part of the University Grounds. On the right of the photograph is the Church of the Redeemer, and in the centre, the sleigh and its driver were busily delivering groceries from Mr. Churchill's Yonge Street store.

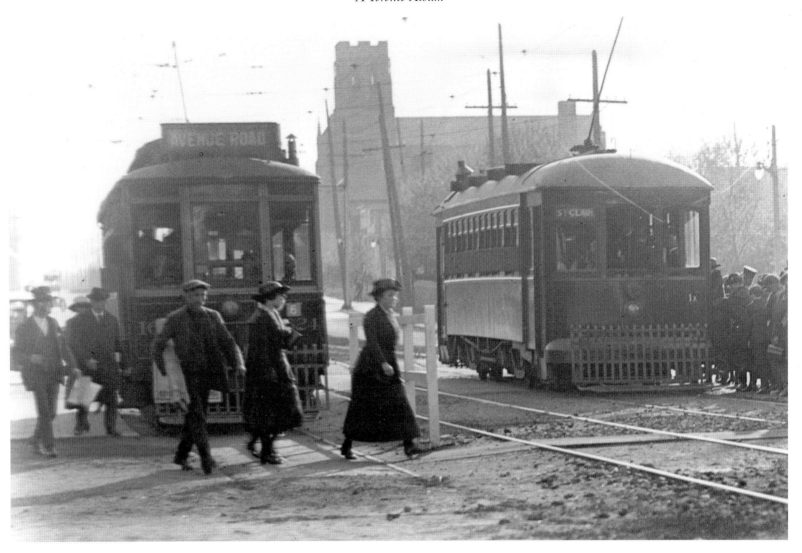

45 The end of the Avenue Road line at St. Clair Avenue, 1916

This view shows homeward-bound passengers changing from a TRC Avenue Road car to a St. Clair car operated by the Toronto Civic Railway. The TRC lines were built and operated by the city in suburban areas not served by the privately-owned TRC. In the misty distance is Timothy Eaton Memorial Church.

The houses built in the Avenue Road, St. Clair, and Rosedale districts had helped to give Toronto its reputation as a "city of beautiful homes." It was described in a contemporary magazine article thus: "No city of equal size in America contains as many substantial and artistic homes and so delightful a series of residential districts as Toronto. The buildings are all constructed from marble, stone, or brick, not a single frame house of any note in the entire city."

The absence of wooden houses was due to fire regulations rather than to such a uniform desire for splendour among the rich, whose numbers had greatly increased in the prosperous years since 1896, a period of time when the prairie economy had started to grow, the mines of northern Ontario began to produce, immigration increased, and huge quantities of money poured into the city. The difference between rich and poor was becoming very noticeable.

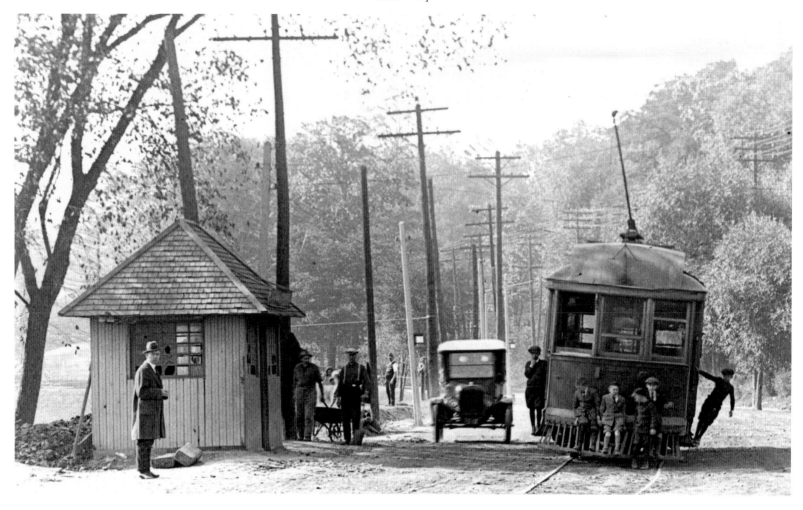

46 Looking west on Davenport Road from Bathurst, 1923

As the city grew, the Toronto Railway Company maintained that its responsibilities did not extend beyond the city limits of 1891, the year its charter began. As a reslt the city-owned Toronto Civic Railway as well as other private companies were formed to run lines in the suburban areas and beyond. One of the latter was the Toronto Suburban Railway (TSR) which was established in 1894. It operated several lines spreading out from the Toronto Junction part of the city. One line ran to Weston, and later on to Woodbridge, while another served the Lambton district. By 1917,

this line had been extended all the way to Guelph. (The Ontario Electric Railway Historical Association's museum near Rockwood is located on the right-of-way of this once-busy line.) A third line of the TSR ran along Davenport Road through the communities of Carlton, Davenport, and Bracondale to Bathurst Street. In 1923, if passengers wanted to travel into the city, they had to walk south to board streetcars of the two-year-old Toronto Transportation Commission (TTC) at Dupont and Bathurst. The TTC absorbed the various TSR lines later that same

year. To the left of the view, down behind the little waiting room, was the Hillcrest racetrack on land shortly to be acquired by the TTC. On it the Commission would erect its extensive Hillcrest shops that opened in 1925.

What was described as the TTC's Hillcrest facility is now the D.W. Harvey Shops (after the Commission's general manager from 1924-1938) with the new David Gunn Building (TTC's Chief General Manager from 1995-1999) on the southwest corner of Bathurst St. and Davenport Rd.

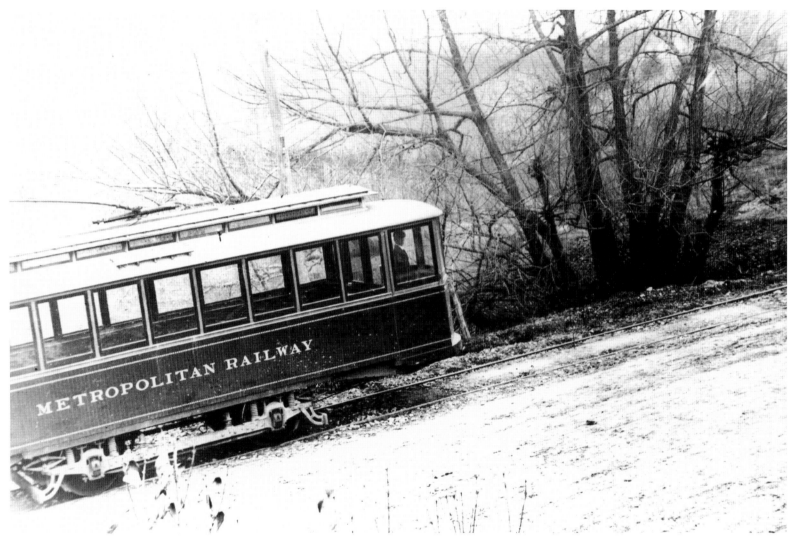

47 A streetcar heading north up (Mount Pleasant) Cemetery Hill on Yonge Street, c1899

In 1885, construction began on a street railway that ran, as a single track with passing sidings, north on Yonge Street from near Summerhill Avenue. The line's first terminal was at the rural community of Eglinton. It was then extended to Richmond Hill and in 1899 to Newmarket. Next Jackson's Point on Lake Simcoe became the end of the line with a further extension to Sutton in 1907. At the turn-of-the-century there were five trips daily to Newmarket at a fare of $1.25 return.

The line had been electrified in 1889 and operated by the Metropolitan Electric Railway Company. After being acquired in 1904 by William Mackenzie and added to his power and railway empire, the company name was changed to the Toronto and York Radial Railway Company. When Mackenzie's empire collapsed, the line was taken over by Toronto with the section north of the city limits operated by Ontario Hydro until 1927. Operations were then turned over to the

Toronto Transportation Commission. Picnic excursions and Sunday school outings were made to the park at Bond Lake until 1930, when the line was closed north of Richmond Hill. Radial cars ran from the city limits to Richmond Hill until 1948 when all north Yonge streetcar service ended.

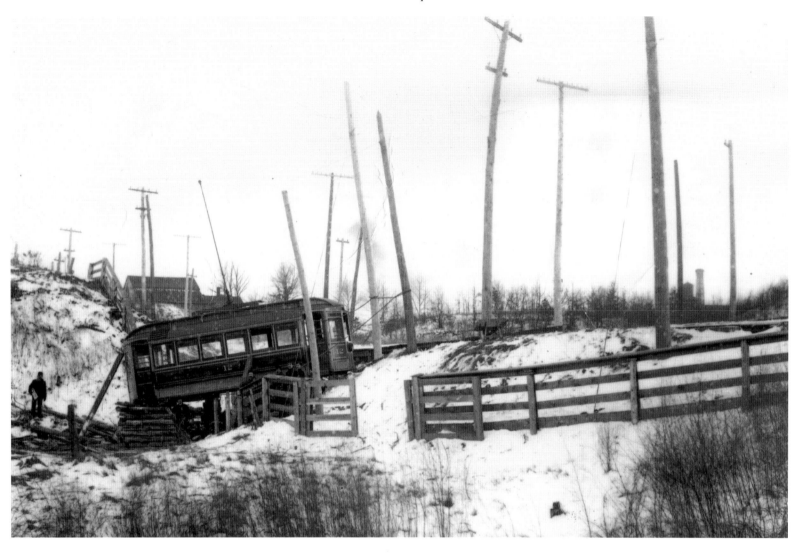

48 A TSR Weston-bound streetcar off the tracks behind Swift's plant, 1907

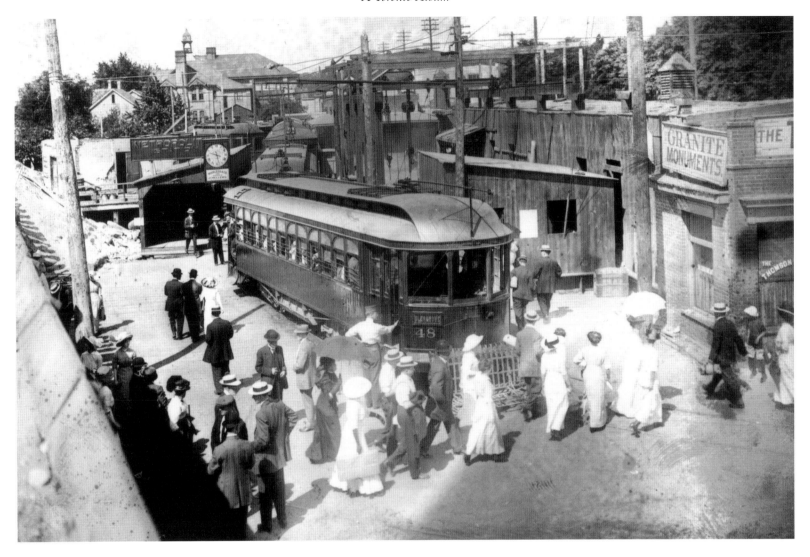

49 The Toronto and York Radial terminus near Birch and Yonge, 1912

The first fifteen or so years of the twentieth century saw the construction of many hundreds of miles of electric railway track, both here in Canada and in the United States. From St. Catharines, one could travel on these lines as far south as Kentucky or as far west as Illinois. But the Hamilton system did not connect to the St. Catharines system, and the Toronto network did not link up with that serving Hamilton, though such connections had frequently been discussed. In 1912, there were some 137 miles of track radiating out from Toronto, and the streetcars that used them were naturally enough called radial cars. These vehicles were larger than the city streetcars and could travel, air horns blaring, at fifty miles an hour.

After the First World War, Ontario Hydro proposed a radial system for Toronto that would bring together many of the existing lines under one operating authority. These lines would travel along the city's waterfront, turn north up Bay Street in to a tunnel leading to a huge terminal located at City Hall. The Ontario government, however, would not guarantee the huge bond issue and the grandiose scheme was doomed.

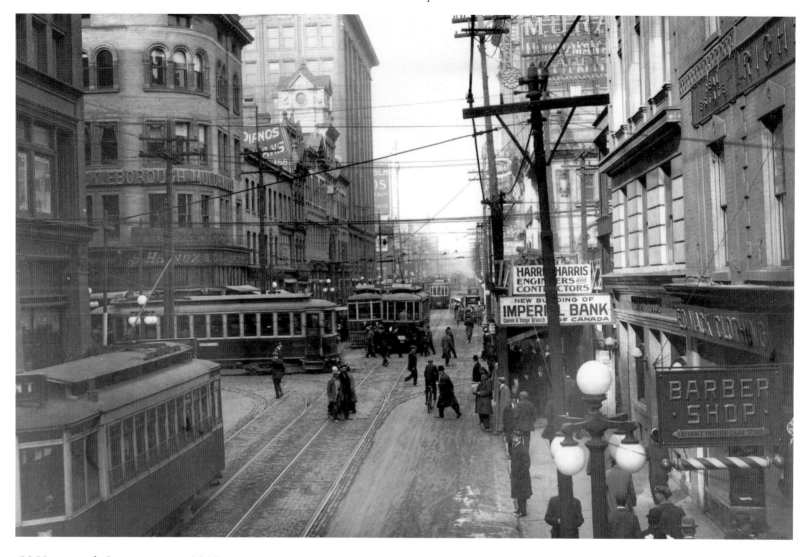

50 Yonge and Queen streets, 1915

The financial and commercial success of the city was further encouraged by the increasing use of telephones and typewriters. The "office revolution" had begun, and the demand for downtown space forced an alteration in the by-laws governing the height and size of buildings. The coherent outer appearance of the old centre city gave way to a complex inner order of office organization within individual buildings; there was economic effi-ciency within, but visual chaos without.

Streetcars brought people in from ever more distant suburbs to their work in ever higher buildings erected on lots and streets tnot intended for such skyscrapers. Eaton's and Simpson's faced one another, and Yonge Street had become the main retail street of the city. Knox's small "Five and Ten" store was eventually replaced by a huge Woolworth store on the same corner.

By this time, the centre of Toronto was beginning to look like an American city. Its ambition, as D.C. Masters said in his book *The Rise of Toronto,* was now to become "less and less unlike New York."

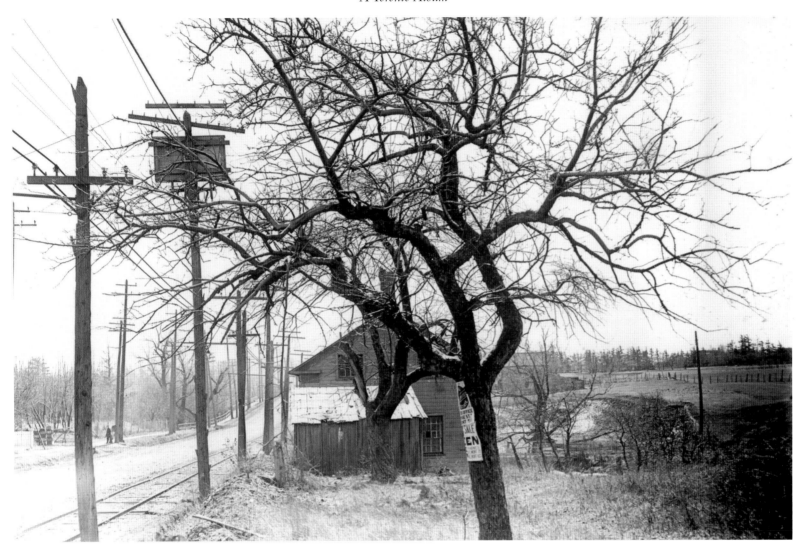

51 Yonge Street near Lawrence Avenue, 1910

Five miles to the north of Queen and Yonge
lay farming country, traversed by the Yonge
Street line of the Toronto and York Radial
line. Now completely urban, this area is about
to be served by an extension of the Toronto
Transit Commission's Yonge Street subway.

*The extension of the Yonge subway from the origi-
nal northern terminus at Eglinton to the new York
Mills station took place on March 31, 1973, and
to Finch one year later.*

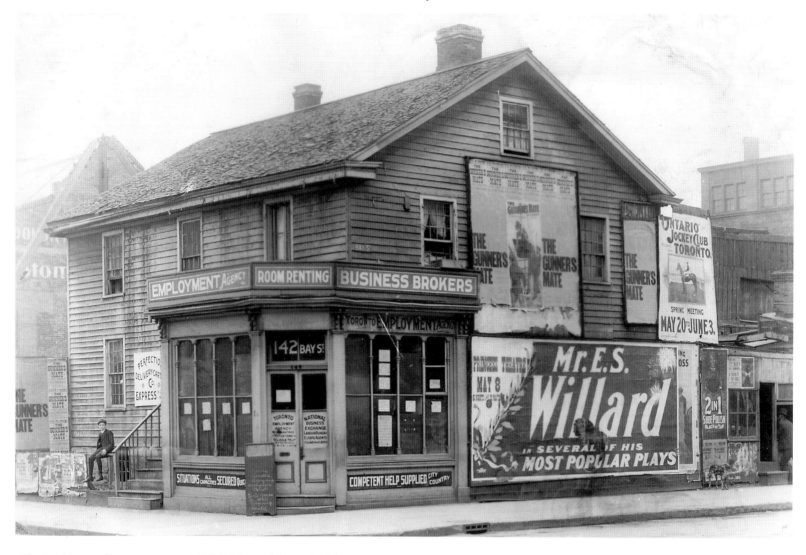

52 At the northwest corner of Adelaide and Bay, 1910

The intensification of commercial life was brought about by the phone, the filing cabinet, the duplicating machine, truck transport, more purchasing power, financial mergers, and so on. These advancements also resulted in the proliferation of outdoor advertisements. Here, the Toronto Employment Agency was advertising for workers, including farm hands.

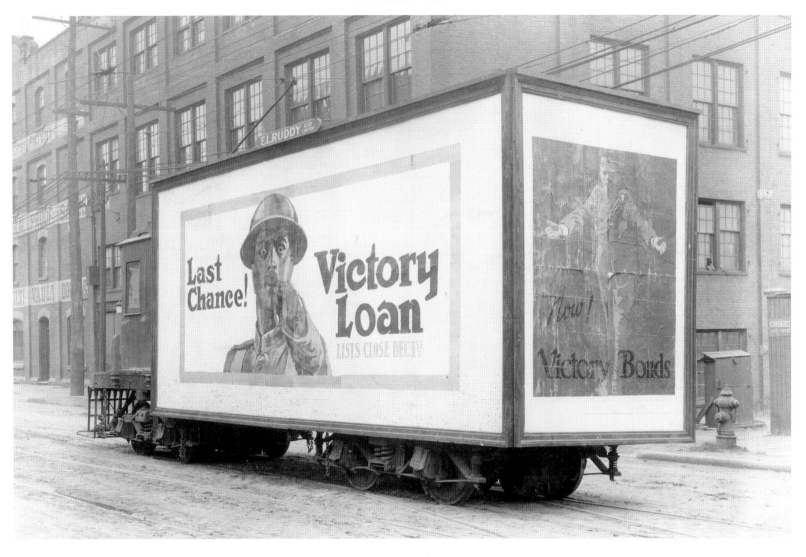

53 TRC workcar and Victory Bond billboard

The outbreak of the First World War did not cause the same patriotic outburst as the South African War had done. This time, "the great tragedy was met with seriousness and resolution." The Exhibition buildings and grounds were used as a "boot camp" to which volunteers and militia came for organization and training, and the American Legion was raised for men who came across the border anxious to fight. Women knitted socks in public, and bridge parties gave way to "bandage socials." The city again insured the lives of all its citizens who went to fight. Torontonians gave some $20 million to various war charities as well as contributing above the national average to the federal bond issues in the latter years of the war. On Armistice Day, November 11, 1918, there was an impromptu carnival with a huge bonfire at Queen and Bay, spontaneous processions and bands, singing in the foyers of hotels, and dancing in the streets. A steam whistle installed in the bell tower of City Hall blared while ticker tape floating all over Bay Street.

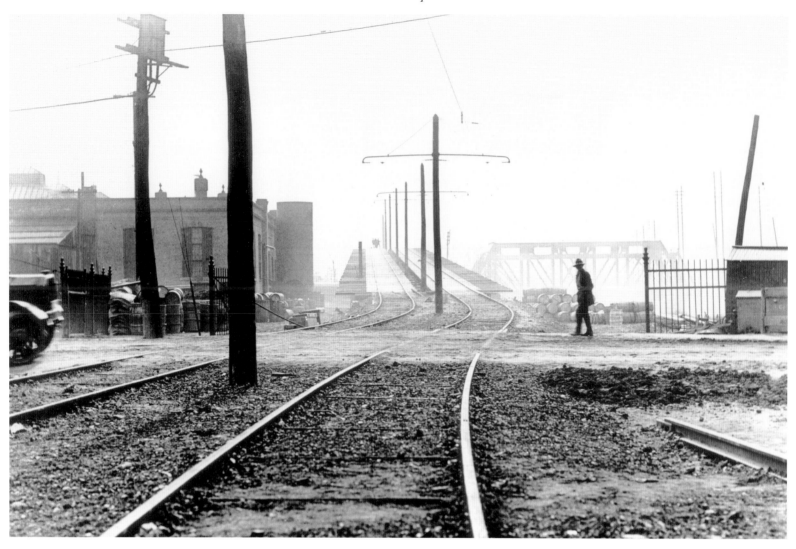

54 The Ashbridge's Bay line: looking south ...

The streetcar line from Queen Street into the developing factories of the "Eastern Harbour Terminals" was carried over the Grand Trunk tracks on the east bank of the Don River by a temporary trestle, seen here from Eastern Avenue and in the next photograph from the present Keating Street. An ice-jam had flooded the Don, in the second photograph, in spite of the draining and canalization of its lower reaches towards the end of the nineteenth century to create industrial land, purify the water, and prevent "ever and ague." These wintry scenes have a bleak harshness to them.

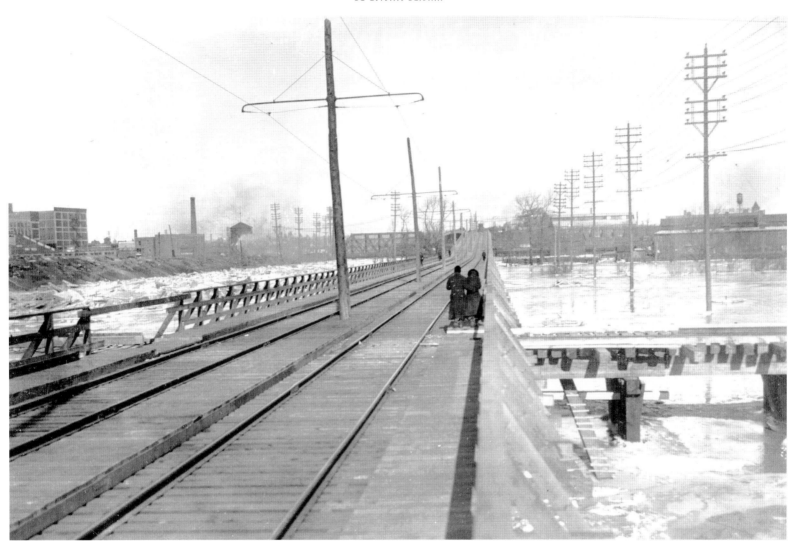

55 ... and looking north, 1917

Among the characteristics that Toronto boasted of in 1917 were: the annual CNE with its National Motor Show, mammoth Exhibition Grandstand, and Women's Building with its 18,500 feet of exhibit space; the number of people "engaged in the culture of gardens ... [whose] work is conducted along artistic lines"; the number of birdhouses in the city's many gardens; the Canadian Society for the Protection of Birds; the cultivation of vacant lots by returned wounded soldiers; "ten church organs with four manuals"; the Mendelssohn Choir; "more musical instruments in the houses of the people than any other city in the world"; the low death rate compared with U.S. cities; a telegram from the King to "Mr. Jos. Seagram, on his winning of the King's Plate for the fifteenth time at the Woodbine Races," and exciting plans to turn the old Don jail into an aquarium.

These two views show land that ninety-one years later was to be part of the 2008 Olympic Games site had the Toronto bid been successful.

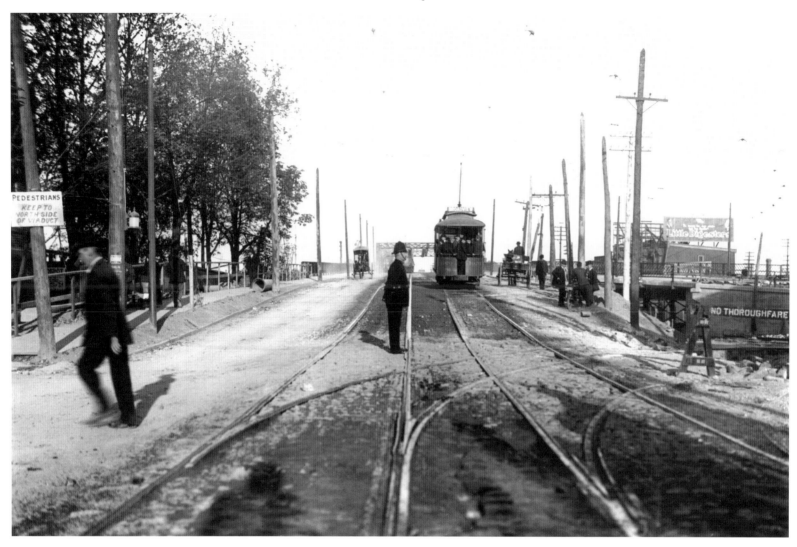

56 Looking east to the new Queen Street bridge, 1911

With so many of its young men in uniform the start of the First World War greatly depressed economic life in Toronto. But after a while, when numerous war contracts started coming in, the city's business life recovered and flourished to such an extent that the TRC cars became even more overcrowded. War industries had first claim on steel, so track deteriorated and, despite court orders, no new cars were built. With doubtless infuriating humour, the Company explained that "the tracks are in the ground in the form of unmined iron ore; and the electrical equipment will be manufactured with all speed as soon as it is ordered." Mackenzie's franchise was drawing to a close. More important was the fact that by 1916 the one-time business tycoon was in deep financial trouble as a result of his failed attempts to turn his beloved Canadian Northern into a transcontinental railway.

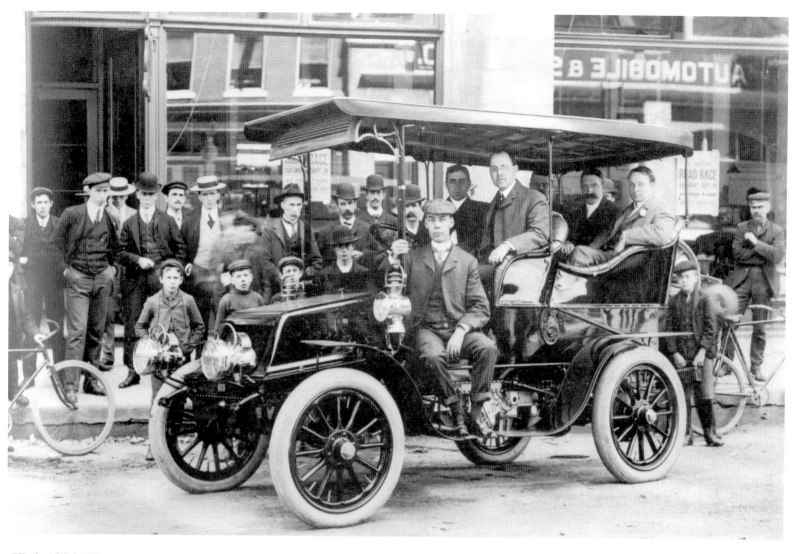

57 A 1904 Winton on Bay Street

Motor manufacturing in Toronto dated back to 1899 when the Canada Cycle and Motor Company (CCM) built a number of small motor tricycles and quadricycles for the post office. Though awkward in design, these single-cylinder, air-cooled machines performed creditably. The following year, electric vehicles were manufactured by a Yonge Street company and in 1905 CCM (later the Russell Motor Car Company) produced a two-cylinder passenger car known as the Russell Model "A."

The poor public transportation service and the prosperity of wartime induced what planners now call a "modal shift." More and more people bought cars resulting in most of the city streets being paved or asphalted. What had been a rather sporting rarity, automobiles became more and more common. This fact quickly put an economic squeeze on the spread of streetcar lines as well as on the operation of the radials. This condition was not felt by society as a whole. Indeed, the automobile gave many people a new, exciting, and comfortable mobility.

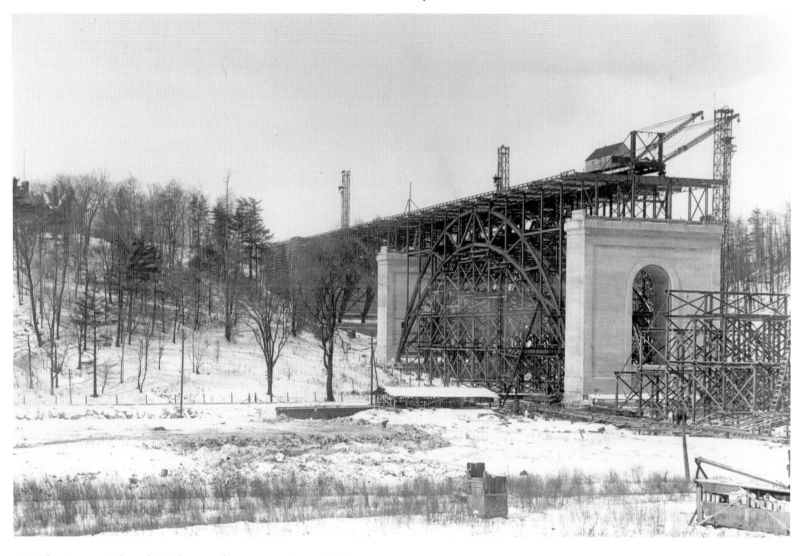

58 The Prince Edward Viaduct under construction, 1916

In 1909, a planning report had recommended that a bridge be built across the Don in the Castle Frank area, with the west end connected by an avenue running diagonally into the downtown part of the city. This latter thoroughfare was never built, and Toronto maintained its square grid street pattern. The bridge to the Danforth was constructed between 1915 and 1918 at a cost of $2 million. Bloor Street was extended from Sherbourne to meet it. The idea of rapid transit was "in the air" at the time, and Jacob and Davies, consulting engineers from New York, recommended that the city build a tube (subway) system, and that openings for the trains be incorporated in the design of the proposed viaduct. They were, but no subway trains passed through them for almost fifty years until the first Bloor-Danforth trains ran in 1966.

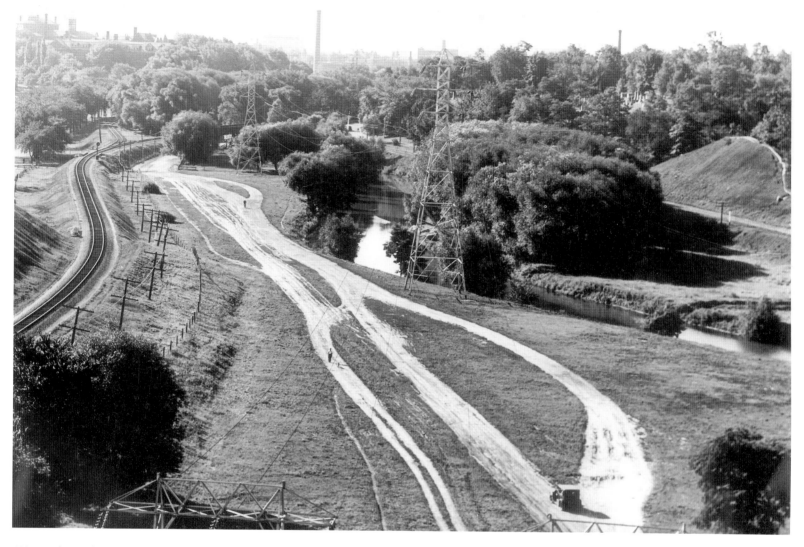

59 Looking down the Don Valley from the new Prince Edward Viaduct, no date

While the complex of dirt tracks may fore-shadow the Don Valley Parkway that would be built through this valley in the 1960s, there were already intruders, a hydro right of way, and two railway lines. The most obvious of this trio is the track put through by the Canadian Pacific Railway when it was permitted to enter the city in 1889. On the far right of this photo, and far less obvious, is the track of that curious turn-of-the-century enterprise, the Belt Line Railway. In 1891, its promoters published a promotional booklet entitled *The Highlands of Toronto* which was graced with charming line drawings of a little steam train tootling merri-ly through the Sylvan scenery of the Don Valley, and the pastoral countryside of what is now Moore Park and Forest Hill. The promot-ers also, as it happened owned a large amount of real estate throughout the "highlands." It was intended that the Belt Line would allow Torontonians to work downtown while living in gracious mansions in a new salubrious envi-ronment. A loop with a similar purpose was later built out towards the Humber River. The brochure concluded by declaring: "The great-est rewards of commerce are won by shrew conjecture of coming events ... Thinking pays!" Unfortunately for all, the land boom soon col-lapsed and the promoters quickly found them-selves in financial trouble. The line operated for a little more than two years before it was taken over by the Grand Trunk Railway and was converted to a freight operation.

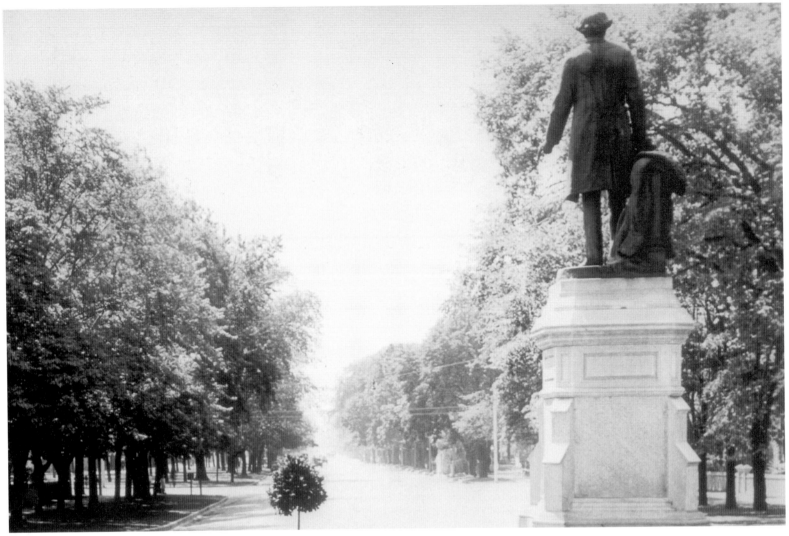

60 Looking south on University Avenue, 1914

Little needs to be said of this most Parisian of Toronto scenes. The statue of Sir John A. Macdonald in front of the Ontario Parliament Buildings, which officially opened in 1893, now gazes down an almost tree-less University Avenue.

61 Looking north on University Avenue from Queen, c1930

The monument commemorates the Canadians who died in the South African War. It was designed by W.S. Allward, a Toronto-trained sculptor who was also responsible for the Soldiers' Memorial at Vimy Ridge. The steel frame of the Canada Life Insurance Company's new office building, the first of the University Avenue towers, was quickly taking shape behind wooden hoardings just to the left of the photo. Despite the good intentions of regulations put in place to govern the look of the office blocks and hospitals proposed for University Avenue, it is hard to believe that what was built improved the street in any way. The value of a beautiful street, avenue, or square is not easily measurable.

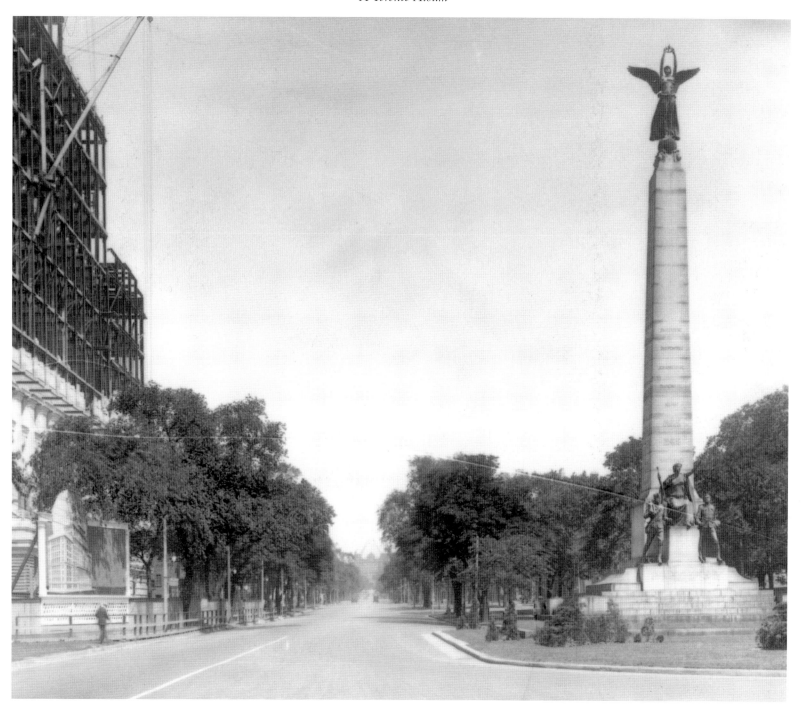

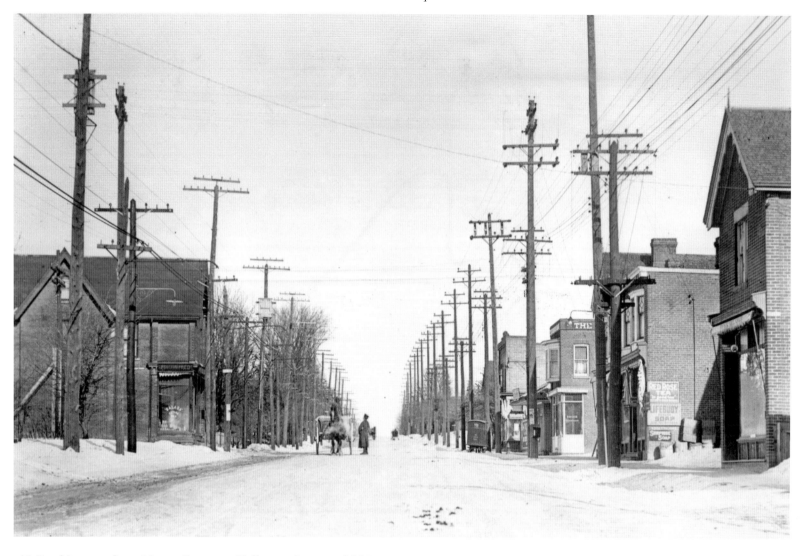

62 Looking north on Yonge Street at Eglinton Avenue, 1917

Eglinton Avenue crossed Yonge as nothing more than a dusty trail. It can be seen in this view just in front of the structure on the left. At this time, the old building was the site of Mr. Coon's feed store. Later it became the Eglinton Restaurant. When the intersection was widened about 1922, the building was physically moved ten or so feet to the northwest. The streetcar track on the left of the photo (barely visible as a dark band in the white snow) is that of the Toronto and York Radial on which Eglinton was identified simply as "Stop 12."

The expansion of the city's boundaries in the 1880s, excessive though it seemed to some at the time, had provided room for development for no more than twenty years. During the period 1903–1914 the city embarked on a second period of growth, this time absorbing another 10,000 acres, including the area in and around the community of Eglinton. This action resulted in Toronto doubling its size once again. And again protests were voiced concerning the tax burden inherent in the servicing of areas with only seven people to the acre. The building of houses was somewhat slowed during the First World War, but in the early 1920s there was rapid development of bungalows in the west end, in the Danforth and Birchcliff areas, and later, in the districts in north Toronto.

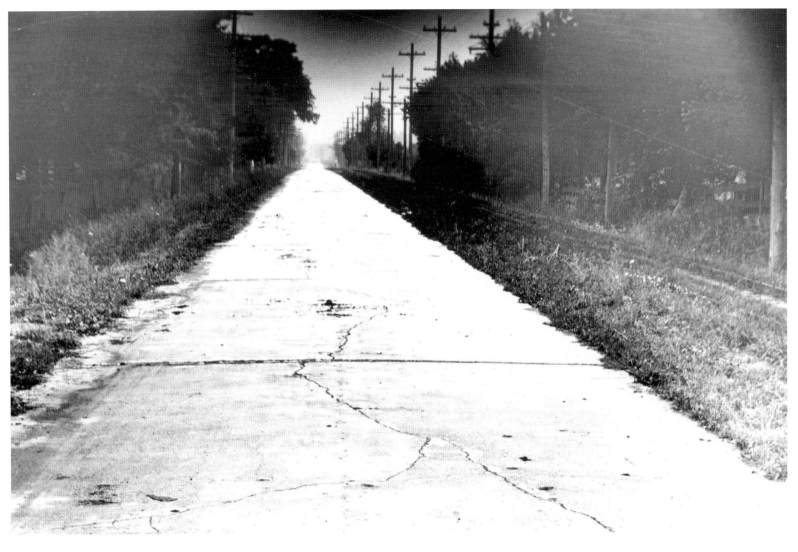

63 The new road to Hamilton, Lakeshore Road, 1916

This unprepossessing vista was one of the minor wonders of its age. It shows one of the longest intercity stretches of concrete in the world, and the first poured-concrete slab highway in Ontario. It is the Lakeshore Road somewhere on the Toronto side of Port Credit, a fact substantiated by the presence of the street railway track on the right that belonged to the Toronto and York Radial Railway (Mimico Division) that went no further. While a similar radial line from Hamilton reached as far east as Oakville, the two were never joined.

In the early 1920s, the Toronto Publicity Bureau published *On to Toronto* by Motor that listed some early traffic regulations to be followed while driving in the City of Toronto: "No horse or vehicle shall be left in such a manner as to obstruct the ordinary traffic of the street ... Overtaking [vehicles] shall give audible warning and pass to the left ... [and, rather confusingly] When any vehicle meets or overtakes a streetcar operated in or near the centre of the travelled portion of the highway which is stationary for the purpose of taking on or discharging passengers, the vehicle shall not pass the car or approach nearer than six feet measured back or forward from the rear or front end, as the case may be, of the car on the side of which passengers are getting on or off until such passengers have got on or got safely to the side of the street, as the case may be."

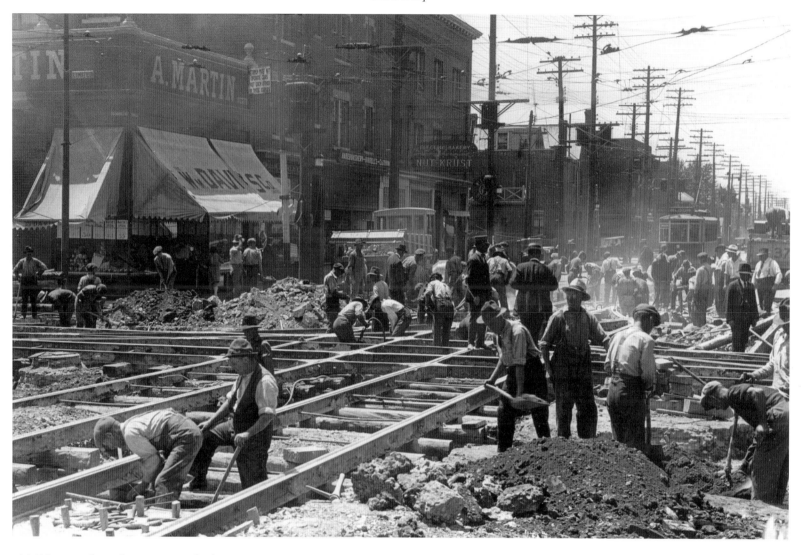

64 Bloor and Bathurst streets looking west, 1922

In 1921, the TRC's franchise finally came to an end. This time disgruntled city fathers had no intention of renewing it or offering it to another entrepreneur. Private enterprise had failed, so public enterprise was to be given its chance. The Toronto Transportation Commission was established and purchased most of the assets of the TRC (after much wrangling) for more than $11 million. Work crews of the new TTC set to work with vigour just as the TRC had done thirty years earlier. Track gangs were soon seen all over the city rebuilding old track and laying new, this time on cement foundations covered with various tamping materials and cushions. On this were laid 6" x 8" x 8' ties to which the track was bolted. Granite block setts paved the street. The track was 4' 10" wide, with a "devilstrip" (the width between two pairs of tracks) of 5' 4". The miles of track increased from 127 to 222 by the end of 1923 (but only to 285 by the end of 1952). The houses seen in the background of this photo were taken over by businessman "Honest Ed" Mirvish throughout the 1950s and 1960s.

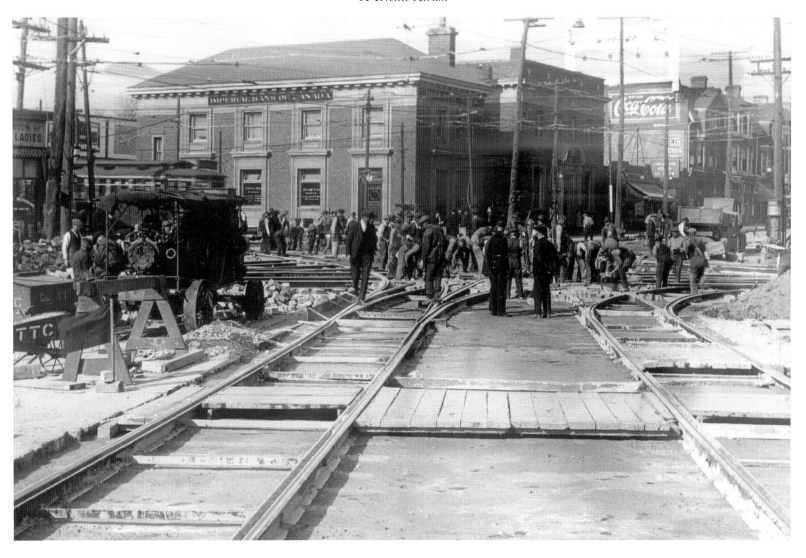

65 Laying new track at King, Queen, Roncesvalles, and Lakeshore Road, 1923

This was the most complicated track inter-section anywhere in the city. Amazingly, all of the old track was removed and new track bolted into place in a mere nine hours. The TTC was overseen by a trio of successful Toronto businessmen known collectively as the Toronto Transportation Commissioners. Under their guidance, the new system was to operate on a service-at-cost basis. Adult fares were set at 7 cents for one ticket (a two cent increase over the TRC's fare structure), 25

cents for four, and $3.00 for fifty. In addition, the transfer system inaugurated by the old TRC was to be continued. The wage rates for motormen and conductors, that is 60 cents an hour after three years of service, time and a quarter on Sundays, time and a half for overtime, was to remain the same for about the next twenty years.

A major rebuilding of this same intersection (plus some extra trackwork) took place in the summer of 2001. This time it took nearly 2 months.

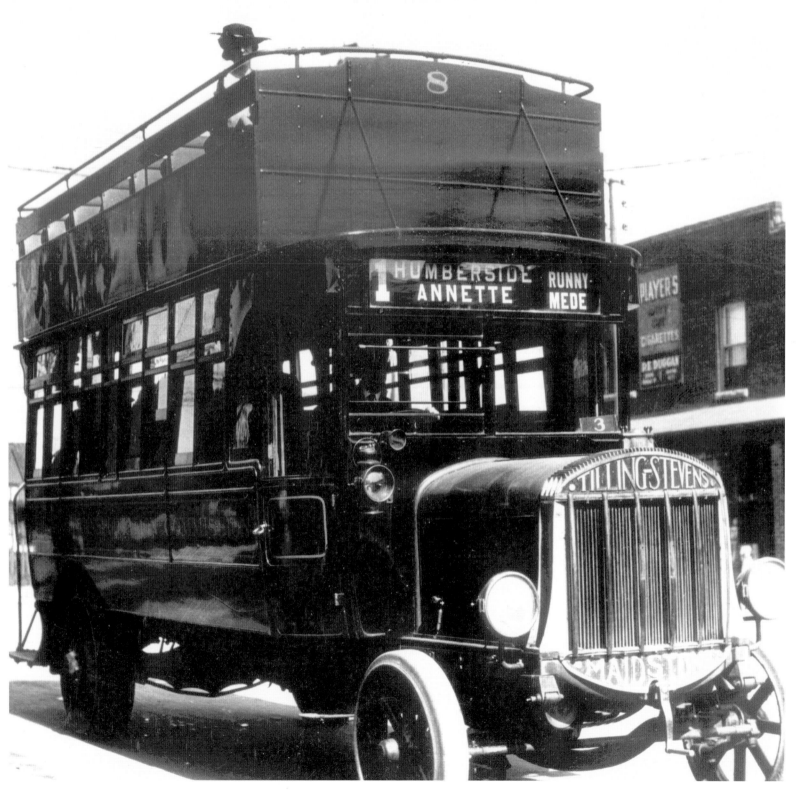

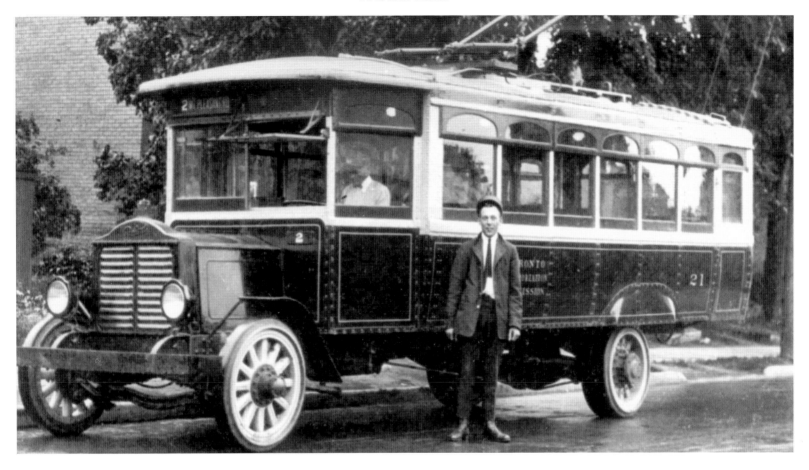

66 TTC double-decker bus, 1922

67 A TTC trolley coach, 1924

The TTC had to replace about half of the streetcars it obtained from the TRC with new vehicles. The Commission had a number of other initiatives including an experiment with this double-deck bus nicknamed "Tilly." It had solid tires and was powered by a gasoline-electric motor. "Tilly" had frequent breakdowns and passengers found riding up top in the winter months too cold. Ultimately, the experiment was considered a failure. The route on which the experiment was tried was a short feeder line to the streetcars on Dundas running via Humberside, High Park, and Annette avenues to Runnymede Road and Dundas.

Another experiment that was tried and not repeated until well after the Second World War was the electric trolley coach. The first models ran from Yonge Street east along Merton Avenue to Mt. Pleasant Road, then north to Eglinton Avenue. These vehicles were taken out of service in 1925 when the streetcars on St. Clair Avenue were extended east to Mt. Pleasant, then north to a loop at Eglinton. Modern trolley coaches returned to Toronto twenty-two years later. A more successful inauguration occurred in 1927 with the incorporation of Gray Coach Lines, a ubsidiary of the TTC that provided an extensive interurban service.

All trolley bus service in Toronto ended in 1993.

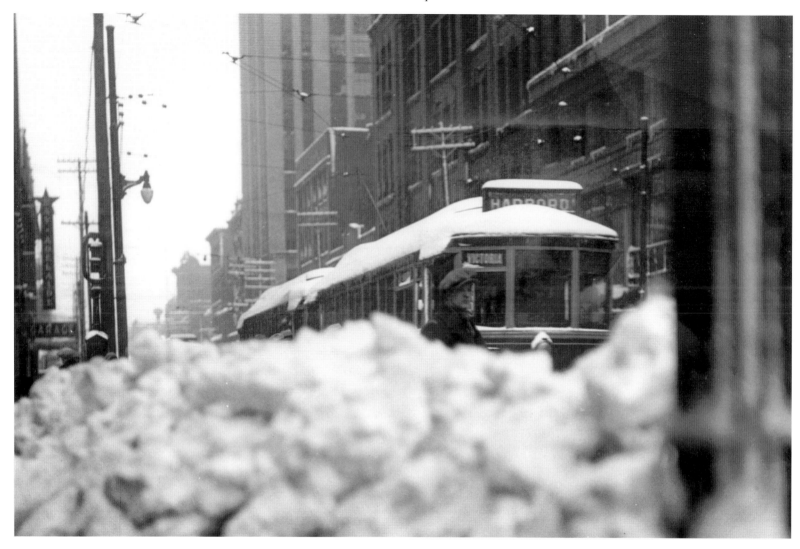

68 After the storm of March 1931 on Adelaide Street

Fifteen inches of heavy wet snow fell during this storm. Many Torontonians will remember a much more severe snowstorm that hit the city thirteen years later. This time twenty-two inches fell in less than twelve hours. Clean-up operations following that storm were much easier than they would be today with war-time restrictions on fuel and tires having ensured that only a limited number of vehicles were around to clog the thoroughfares.

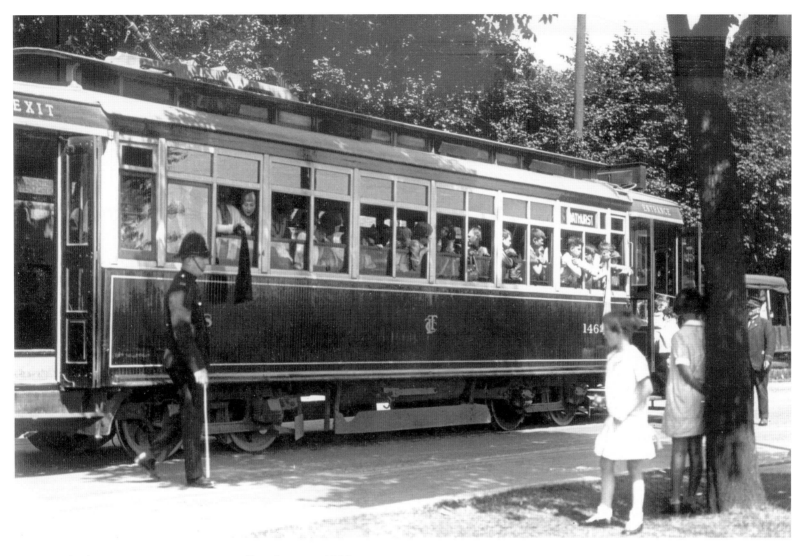

69 Free bathing car, King at Roncesvalles Avenue, 1929

As modern and efficient as the TTC wanted to be, it continued a service, the free bathing car, that had been inaugurated years earlier by its forerunner, the TRC. Actually, the concept harks back to the late nineteenth century when the city provided free passage across the bay for children so they could swim at the Island. On each day of the school holidays, right up until 1929, a fleet of free streetcars ran from various neighbourhoods in the city to Sunnyside Beach and the Island Ferry Docks. There were two supervised beaches on the Island as well as two in the east end of the city, at Simcoe Park (now Cherry Beach), and at Kew Gardens (now Kew Beach). The free bathing car was continued, in a slightly modified form, right into the early 1950s when its popularity wained and the service terminated. Official records from 1930 reveal that what were called "Athletic Grounds" were provided by the city with "reasonable liberality." That year there were, 270 tennis courts, 24 lawn-bowling greens, 77 baseball diamonds, 41 football fields, 10 cricket pitches, 7 lacrosse fields, 2 quoiting grounds; and, for the winter, 65 hockey rinks, 645 skating rinks, 16 winter slides for children, 7 toboggan slides, and 1 curling rink.

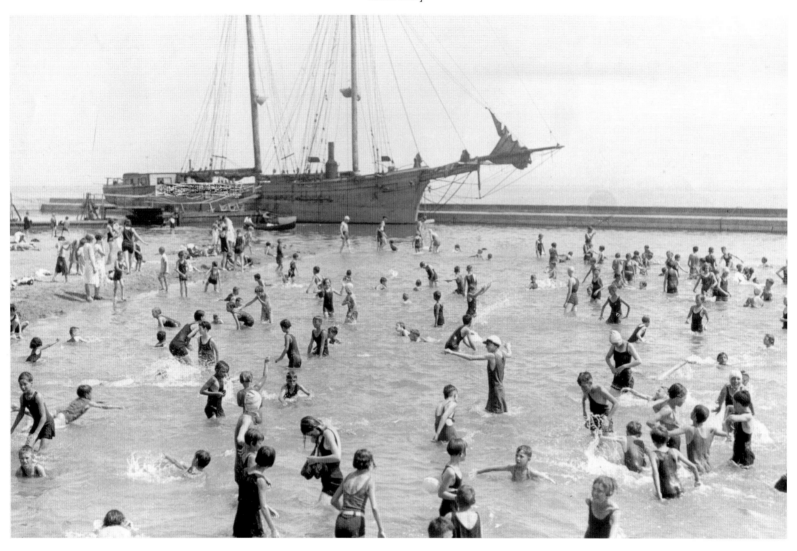

70 At Sunnyside Beach, 1931

After the First World War, the Toronto Harbour Commission began the development of the waterfront from the Humber River eastwards. A concrete breakwall was constructed offshore along the city's western waterfront in order to create a protected passageway between the Humber River and Toronto Harbour for small boats as well as a venue for the popular canoe races. In a report issued by the city it was remarked that "Toronto's citizens love to play and swim and paddle and frolic in the sunshine and fresh air of Canada's healthful climate. They have a keen appreciation of the ideal facilities provided by the city's lakeshore location and the cultivation of natural advantages by municipal enterprise." In the background of this photograph, we see the *Julia B. Merrill*, a lake freighter built in Michigan in 1872. Described as the last wooden sailing ship on the Great Lakes, she was set on fire while moored to the Sunnyside breakwall in an effort to attract crowds to the amusement park.

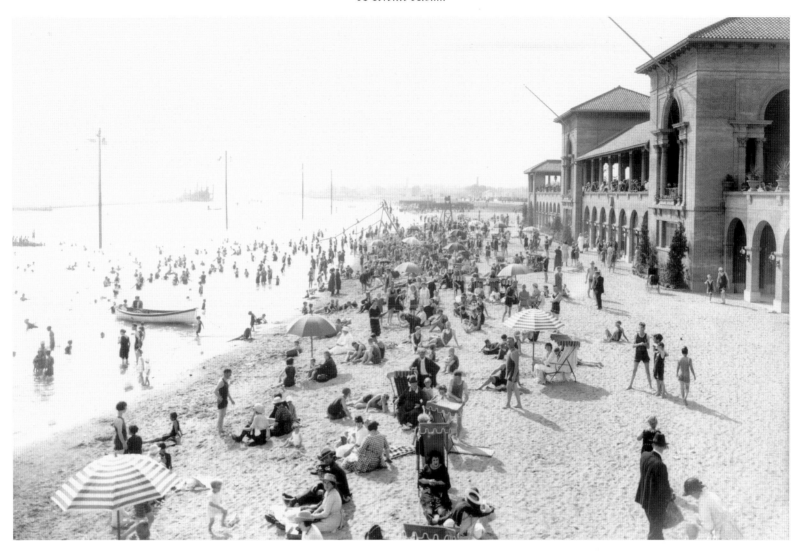

71 Sunnyside Beach in the 1920s

The Bathing Pavilion was built by the Toronto Harbour Commission in 1922 as part of its western beaches development project. The mammoth facility was "equipped with every modern convenience for the comfort and safety of bathers. Close to 8,000 bathers may be accommodated at one time. Water slides for adults and children are provided free of charge and, in the morning, there are free swimming instructions for the children."

The Sunnyside Bathing Pavilion was a far cry from an earlier Toronto bathing establishment known as the "Royal Floating Baths," an attraction that was erected on the water's edge at the foot of Frederick Street in 1836. This one contained ten warm and ten cold baths as well as a promenade deck, drawing room and a reading room. Newspapers of the day hoped to see it "respectably patronized."

The Toronto Harbour Commission also built the Lake Shore Boulevard along the city's western foreshore on land reclaimed from the old Humber Bay. It came complete with a two-mile long, wooden broadwalk promenade along the water's edge.

A small restaurant has recently opened in the old Sunnyside Bathing Pavilion.

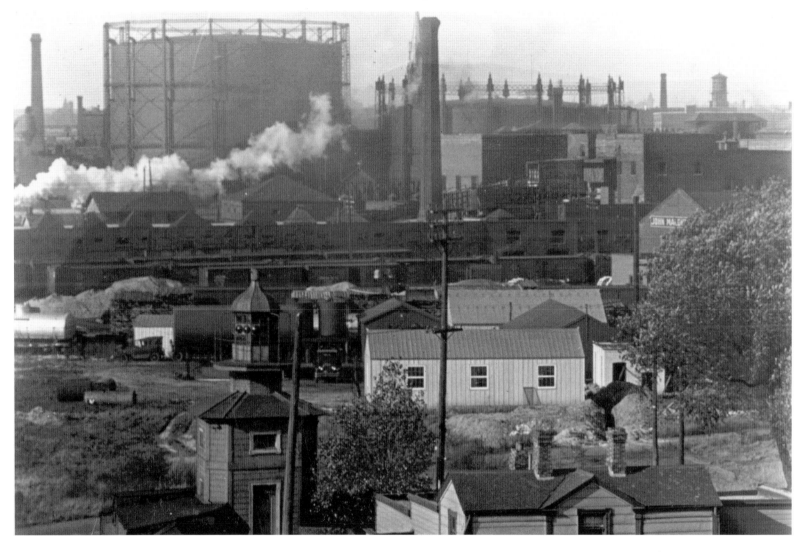

72 Looking north from the "Old Western Gap," 1927

This photograph shows something of the industrial chaos that had developed over the years along Toronto's waterfront. In the foreground are remnants of an earlier waterfront development, the ancient Queen's Wharf lighthouse, and the lightkeeper's house. In the background, on the west side of Bathurst Street, stand two of the Consumers' Gas Company's telescopic storage tanks.

From Bathurst Street east to the Don, the railways and the industries and services that they spawned were cluttered in smoky profusion. In 1909, the Toronto Board of Trade asked the city to do something about the harbour, since it was no longer adequate for the handling of larger vessels and the ever-increasing volume of traded merchandise. At that time, the land adjacent to the harbour was owned by the railways, a myriad of private individuals and enterprises, the old Harbour Commission, and the city itself. As a result it was extrememly difficult to get a consensus on any planned harbour improvements. The situation was untenable and eventually the city asked the federal government to appoint a new Board of Harbour Commissioners. This was done and all the land in question was transferred to it. The "control and development" of Toronto's harbour and its waterfront was now in the hands of the new Toronto Harbour Commission.

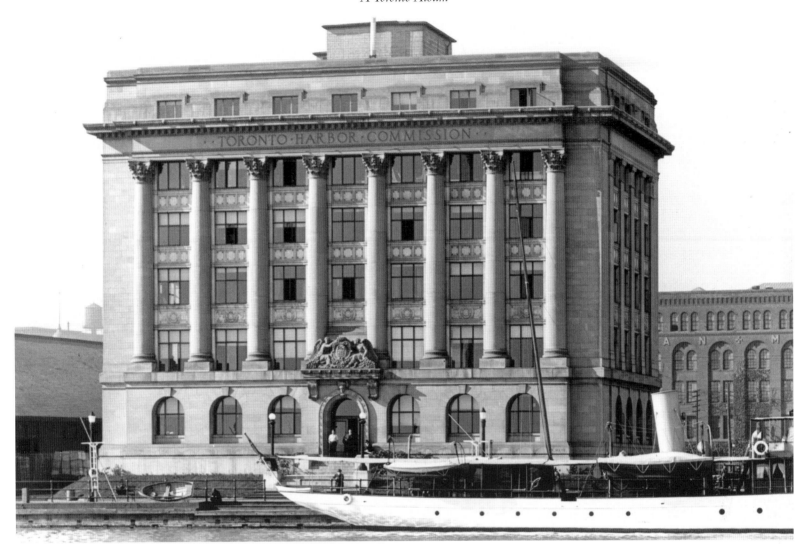

73 Toronto Harbour Commission Building, c1920

The Commission's new administration building, constructed of "reinforced concrete with decorative pillars", opened in May 1918 right at the water's edge on new land that had been reclaimed from the harbour. Moored in front of the beautiful building is the Commission's steam yacht, *Bethalma,* that was used to show off harbour redevelopments to prospective customers. The Commission quickly established new dockage and industrial areas, not just within the harbour proper, but also throughout what had formerly been marsh to the east, known as Ashbridge's Bay. Two classes of society, it was said, had been interested in this area, duck hunters and landgrabbers. The latter were unable to persuade the city that they could do what was necessary to make these 2,000 acres into "the greatest industrial location in North America." This was another reason for creating a new Harbour Commission and giving it wide powers over the way the waterfront was to be used and developed. The new authority's powers extended from the mouth of the Humber to Victoria Park Beach. It also had an Airports Division and went on to build landing facilities at the west end of Toronto Island and out near the little farming community of Malton. The former became Port George VI Island Airport (now Toronto City Centre), and the latter Pearson International.

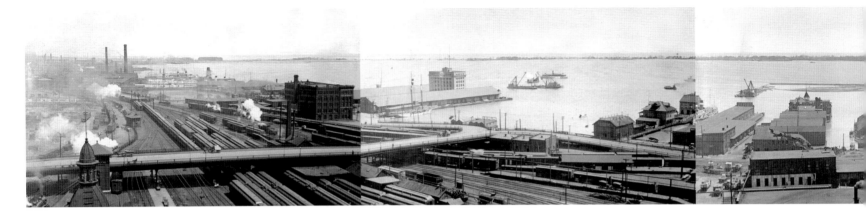

74 The waterfromt 1924

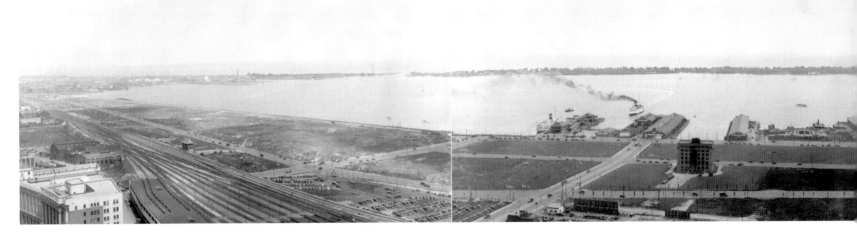

75 The waterfront 1934

These two panoramic views show something of the work carried out by the Toronto Harbour Commission as it reclaimed the harbour to make new industrial land and dock areas along the city's waterfront. Unfortunately, any old landmarks were lost in the process; the Argonaut Rowing Club at the end of the easternmost pier in the top photograph, for example. The top photographs were taken from the clock tower of the old Union Station west of York Street and the view below from the five-year-old Royal York Hotel.

The proliferation of train tracks had begun in the 1850s when steamers and schooners that docked at the Queen's Wharf were met by the latest wonder of the age, the steam locomotive. The first locomotive seen in Toronto was built in Portland, Maine, and called the Lady Elgin, in honour of the wife of the then Governor General of the Province of Canada, James Bruce, 8th Earl of Elgin.

In 1853, James Good's small engineering works, located not far from the Yonge and Queen intersection, produced a locomotive of its own. It was called the Toronto, and powered the first train to operate in what was still known as Upper Canada. It left Toronto for Machell's Corners (now part of Aurora) on May 16, 1853, on the line of the Ontario, Simcoe, and Huron Union Railroad, a company known by its detractors as the "Oats, Straw, and Hay." This company, later to be renamed the Northern Railway of Canada, took possession of the waterfront between

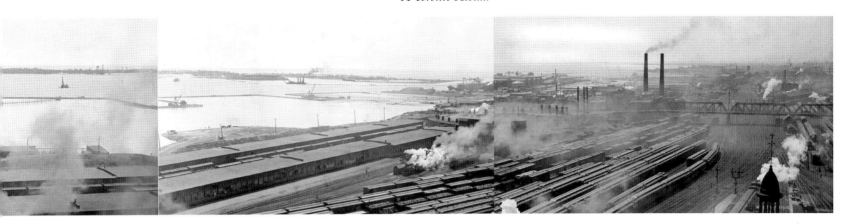

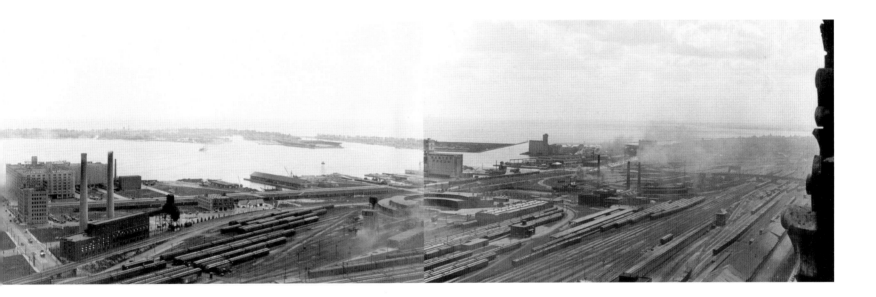

Brock Street (Spadina Avenue) and Queen's Wharf with its passenger station at the foot of Brock. Next came the Great Western Railway that ran its first train to Hamilton in December, 1855. From 1866 it had a terminal at the foot of Yonge Street and a station on the Queen's Wharf. The third railway was the Grand Trunk. Its first train ran to Guelph in July, 1855, and to Montreal in October, 1856. The fourth and fifth railways to serve Toronto, the Toronto and Nipissing, and the Toronto, Grey and Bruce had stations at Berkeley Street and Brock Street, respectively. This excess of stations was corrected as the Grand Trunk began to absorb many of the lines. In 1872, the railway built an imposing station between York and Simcoe Streets. Later, Canadian Pacific trains ran into this station as well. The present Union Station opened in 1927 although full use of the station's facilities wouldn't begin for another three years.

The invasion of the rail companies, drawn to the waterfront like bears to honey, had not been particularly welcomed by the city. For many years, the idea had been that an esplanade for the pleasure of the residents and visitors would one day go run along Toronto's waterfront. The coming of the railways encouraged the city to start building up such a promenade, but the economic and the political power of these companies was such that they simply took over the waterfront. By 1860 young Toronto's dream of becoming a model colonial town, architecturally and perhaps socially as well, was shattered for ever.

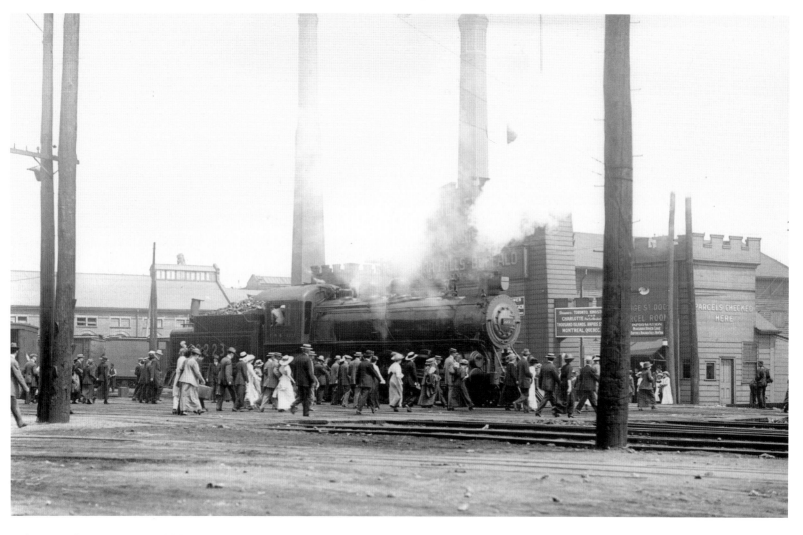

76 Yonge Street crossing, 1912

To reach the island ferries, Torontonians had to cross this proliferation of railway tracks. Up to sixteen pairs of tracks had to be crossed at some streets. In 1907, protests about this inelegant state of affairs were made (but not for the first time), and the city proposed that the lines west from Bathurst to Sunnyside be depressed, and from Sunnyside west to the city limits be raised and bridged over. In addition, it was suggested that all lines, including shunting lines east of Bathurst, be raised on a viaduct. The Federal Board of Railway Commissioners supported the city and the Grand Trunk slowly, but surely did its part to ease the situation in the western areas of the city. The Canadian Pacific, on the other hand, appealed the Board's ruling on the viaduct idea to the Supreme Court. An agreement was eventually reached in 1913 whereby the Canadian Pacific, the Grand Trunk, and the city would share costs equally. Then came the First World War and another series of disagreements with the railways. It wasn't until 1924 that work could begin in earnest.

The implementation of the massive viaduct scheme was important to the outcome of the Toronto Harbour Commission's plans and was a great public controversy in its day. At one point ordinary traffic bridges over the tracks were proposed as an alternative to raising the tracks. In fact, one such bridge was built at the York Street crossing, but the grades were considered too steep for the safe movement of traffic and pedestrians.

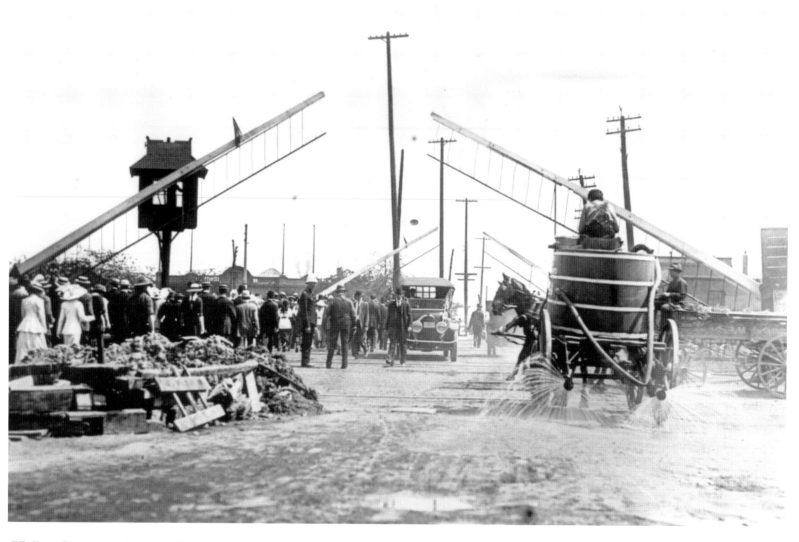

77 Bay Street crossing, 1913

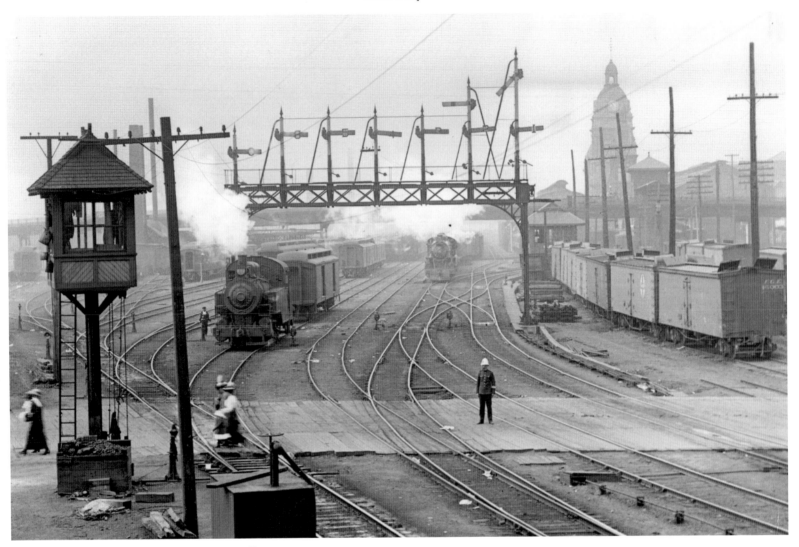

78 One of "Toronto's finest" directs traffic
over the dangerous Bay Street crossing in the spring of 1914

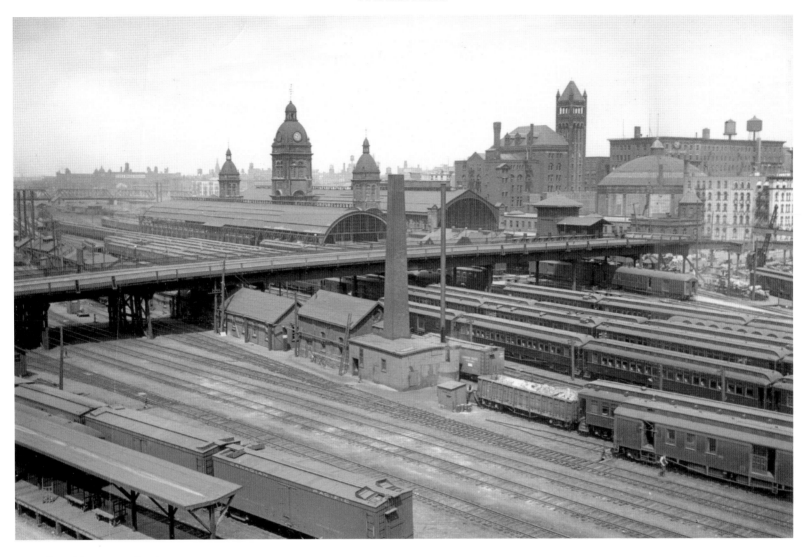

79 The old Union Station

The Grand Trunk called its red, two-storey station building between York and Simcoe streets a "Union" station even before the company had absorbed any of its competitors. Then, in 1872, it erected this three-towered building with train shed to the north. At the official opening, Grand Trunk officials stated that "this building will take care of business for many a long year." However, by 1891 the building was proving inadequate and a new train shed to the south and an attached office "tower" on Front Street were erected by order of the railway's English Board of Directors. The Canadian Pacific Railway began to share these expanded facilities in 1896.

The three-towered structure was built of white brick on its north front, but with all the smoke and soot this "architectural glory" soon faded. In 1885, 500 men on their way to help quell an armed rebellion in the north west led by one Louis Riel, boarded trains at this station as the local militia bands played "Auld Lang Syne" and "The Girl I left Behind Me."

For many years, the voice of GTR Constable George Healy, audible above the hiss of steam, the clang of bells, and the shriek of whistles, boomed out, syllable by syllable, the names, Indian, English, and French of dozens of far-away places across the Dominion.

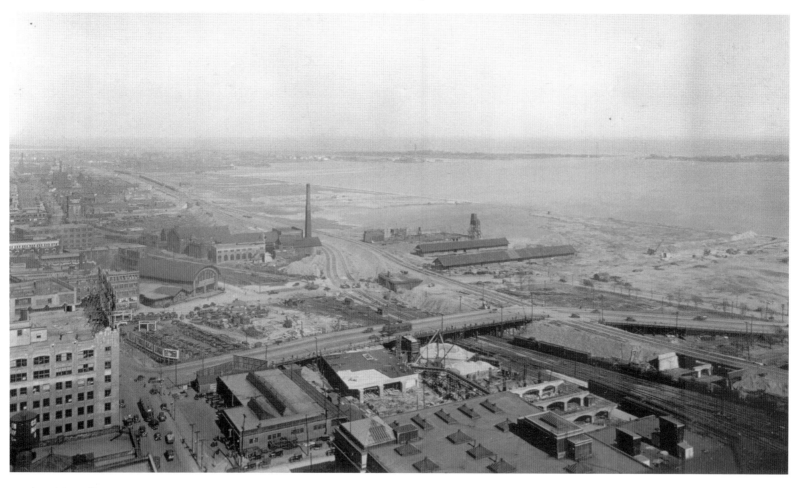

80 Building the railway viaduct, 1929

This scene shows the scale and confusion of the work undertaken by the city and the railway companies, as well as the efforts taken by the former in an attempt to maintain its link with the waterfront and the Island. At the lower right of the view, we can see the roof of the present Union Station. Construction of the massive building began just before the outbreak of the Great War and was all but finished by 1920. The structure was built on the ruins of the Great Toronto Fire of 1904 that swept clean the south side of Front Street between Bay and York. The acquisition of this property by the railways helped trigger the city's demand for an elevated viaduct to end the menace and inconvenience of the level crossings across the city's waterfront as well as a series of grade separations along Bloor and St. Clair in the west. Due to ongoing confusion as to just where the viaduct and its tracks would be placed, Union Station stood empty and unused until 1927 when it was officially opened by the Prince of Wales. The old Union Station was torn down soon after. Full use of the new building didn't come until years later.

At the left of the photograph can be seen the arched roof of the Great Western's railway station that was built at the foot of Yonge Street in the 1860s. The building (as well as the railway) eventually passed into the hands of Canadian National and was used as a fruit depot until destroyed by fire in 1952. The O'Keefe Centre opened on the site eight years later.

In 1996, the O'Keefe Centre for the Performing Arts was renamed the Hummingbird Centre for the Performing Arts following a charitable donation of $5 million from Hummingbird Communications Ltd. to assist with needed capital improvements.

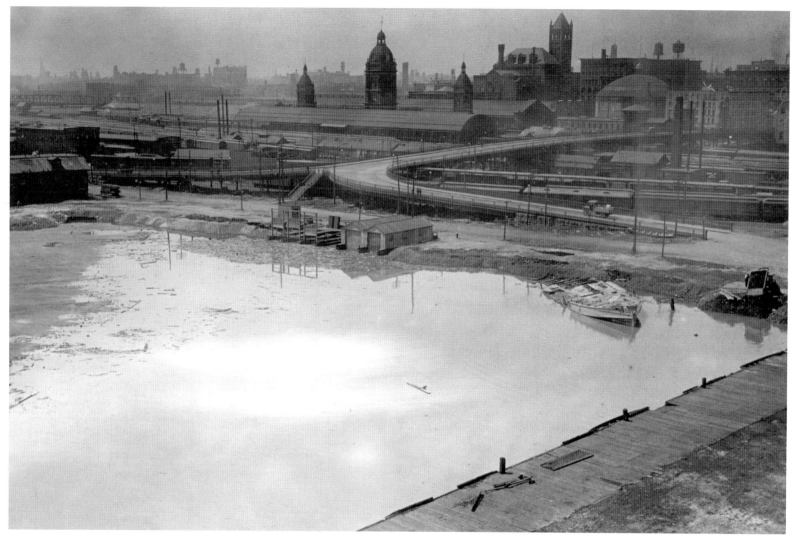

81 Filling in the harbour at the foot of York Street, in the early 1920s

In the 1920s, Toronto began to see itself in very quantitative terms. A Toronto souvenir booklet published in 1926 includes these "Facts About Toronto": "3,521 industries, 560 miles of streets, 216 branches of American industries, 68 parks, 1,978 acres of park area, 40 equipped playgrounds ... 106,360 people employed in manufacturing ... 64% of its citizens own their own homes ... letters sent out from Toronto Post Office annually, approximately 225,000,000 ... site of the Largest Annual Exhibition in the world ... Residential lighting rate averages less than $1.00 per month for six-roomed house ... Best street lighting system in America and at the lowest cost ... (the city) has more capital invested in manufacturing than all the money in the industries of British Columbia, Nova Scotia and New Brunswick combined."

Such materialistic boasting seems unlikely to have won friends or influenced people, unless perhaps, they were American industrialists.

82 Ashbridge's Bay in the 1920s

It looks like a scene from Huckleberry Finn, but the vessel in the background is, in fact, one of the Toronto Harbour Commission's specially designed dredges of which there were three. They could suck and pump between 400 to 1,200 cubic yards per hour of harbour muck, which was then dumped into this willow wilderness, a total of 4 million cubic yards in all. Some 800 acres of this man-made land are now covered with coal dumps, oil tanks, factories, Ontario Hydro's R.L. Hearn thermal generating station, and the Ashbridge's Bay main sewage treatment plant.

Once Ashbridge's Bay was filled in, the displaced ducks began to use the harbour itself as a stopover point in their spring and fall migrations. Wild celery on the bottom of the inlets supported canvasbacks, redheads, and bluebills. It was reported that the black duck had altered its daytime feeding habits and was now scouring the shoreline after sunset in an effort to escape hunters. The couple in the photo were probably fishing for carp.

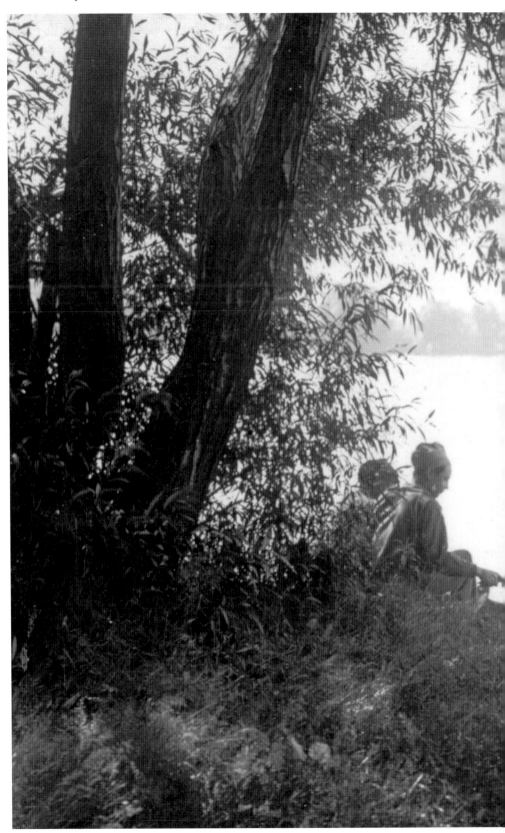

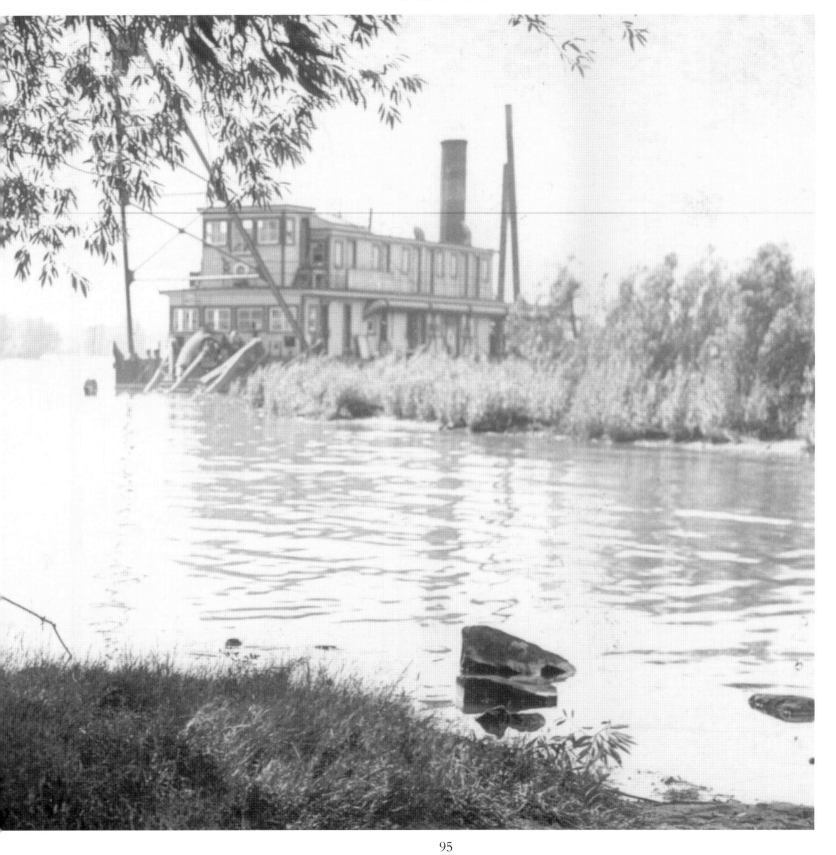

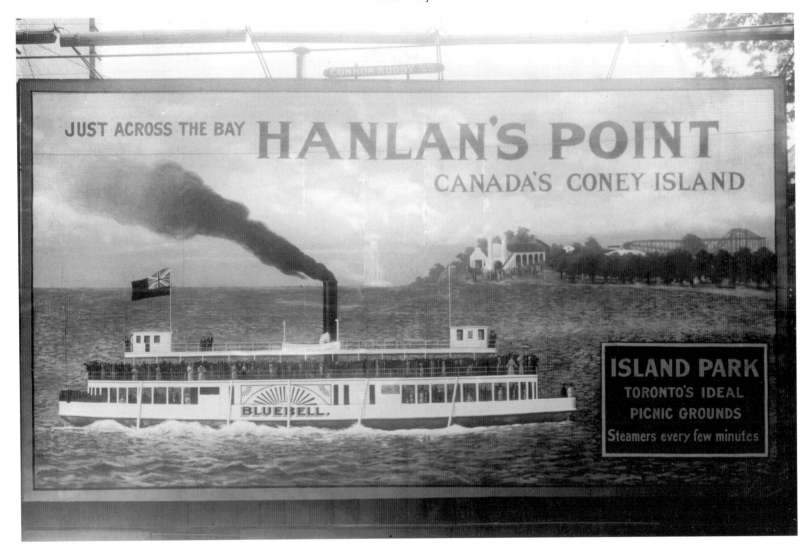

83 An early billboard

The Island ferry *Bluebell* was built in 1906 and its sister *Trillium* in 1910, both for the Toronto Ferry Company. In 1956, *Bluebell* was ignominiously converted into a garbage scow and was employed in an activity no longer performed: the disposing of the city's garbage into the depths of Lake Ontario. *Trillium* still lies beached at Hanlan's Point with hopes of turning her into a museum all but abandoned.

The Toronto Ferry Company came under the control of interests owning the Toronto Baseball Club, whose team played ball at the Hanlan's Point stadium until 1925. The following year a new stadium opened on reclaimed land at the foot of Bathurst Street. Here there was plenty of space for the parking of cars. This stadium has recently been demolished as well. The Toronto Ferry Company was bought by the city in 1926 and

ferry operations turned over to the TTC the following year. In 1960, these operations became the responsibility of the Metropolitan Toronto Parks Department.

After a $1.1 million restoration, the 1910 Toronto Island ferry Trillium *was returned to service in time for the 1977 summer season.*

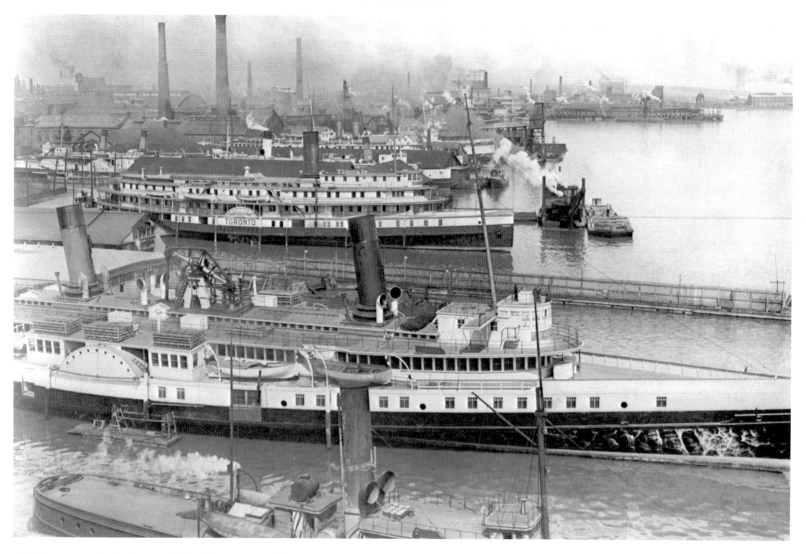

84 Steamers docked east of the Toronto Harbour Commission Building, c1920

The Niagara steamer *Chippewa*, with its unusual "walking-beam" engine, is in the fore-ground. She was built in Hamilton in 1892, and ran the Toronto–Queenston–Lewiston route until laid up in 1936. In the background are the *Toronto* and *Chicora*, the latter a former blockade runner during the American Civil War.

One wonders if air pollution was an accepted sign of prosperity back then?

85 The John Hanlan

This small single-screw steamer, with a capacity of 175 passengers, was in Island ferry service from 1884 to 1928. When burned off Sunnyside the following year some of the spectators actually wept.

86 A captured German submarine in Toronto Harbour, June 1919

The American government sent this trophy of war, *UC97,* on a "goodwill" tour of several of the Great Lakes. The vessel was then taken to Chicago where it was subsequently sunk during a naval gun practice exercise.

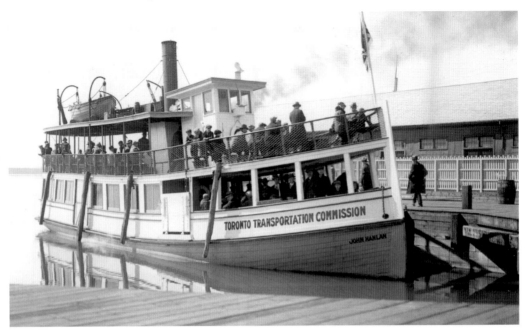

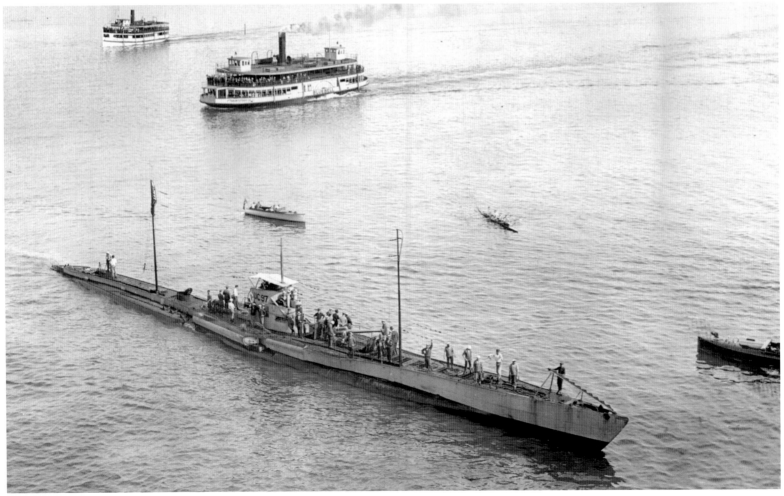

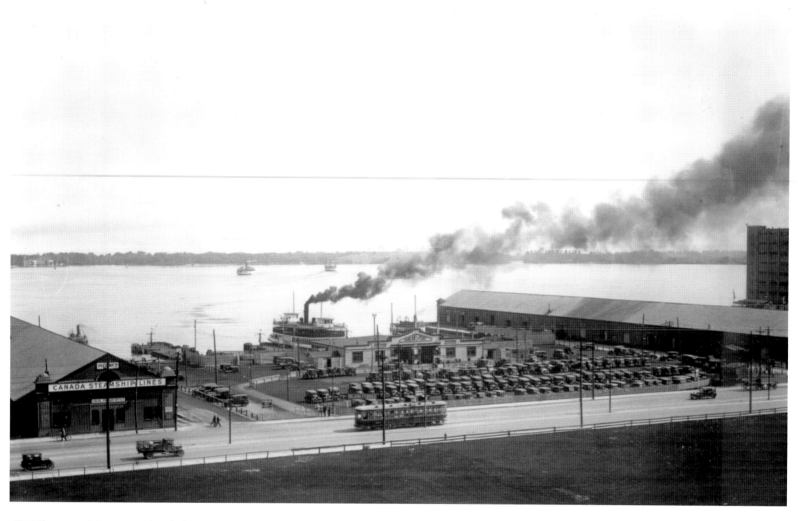

87 The new Toronto Island ferry docks, 1929

The signboards reveal that Hanlan's Point was still the main Island destination in 1929, but by this time it was no longer quite the Mecca of fun it had once been. Over the years, fires had destroyed many of the attractions, and not all had been rebuilt. Despite proposals to incorporate the Island into the city's road system, no bridges or tunnels have ever been completed though several have been suggested. The old saying that public parks served as the city's "lungs" takes on new significance with the present concern over air pollution from automobiles. The parked cars in this photograph look uniformly black, and the TTC "Small Peter Witt" streetcar, in its red and cream livery, must have seemed bright and colourful. The ferry stoking up at the docks is the *Primrose*. In the distance are the *Trillium* and *Bluebell*.

The location of the Toronto Island Ferry Docks was moved to the new Harbour Castle Hilton (now Westin Harbour Castle) at the foot of Bay St. in 1975.

88 Roller rink at Hanlan's Point, 1934

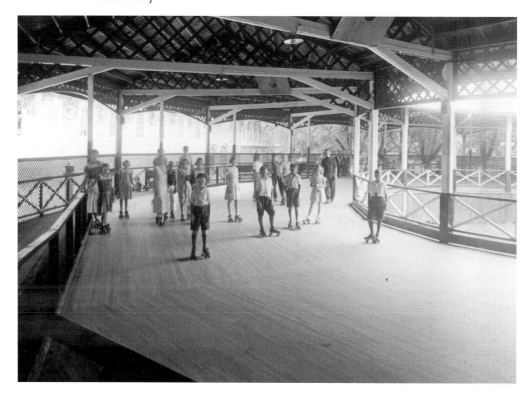

89 Merry-go-round at Hanlan's Point, 1928

"The Western part of Toronto Island is known as Hanlan's Point and has a fine athletic field and a stadium with a seating capacity of 10,000. It also has a fine amusement park and is known for the excellence of its band concerts during the summer season. Adjacent to Hanlan's Point is Centre Island which has a large picnic park as well as many summer hotels and a large number of fine summer residences."

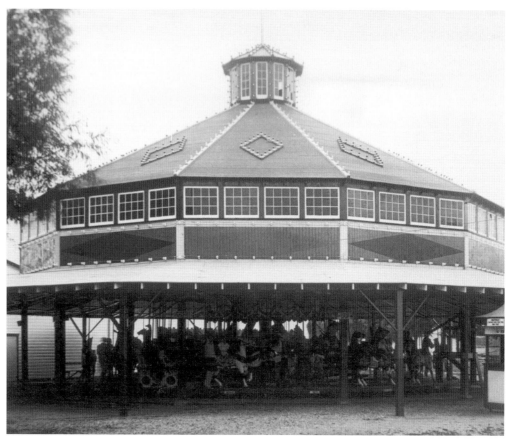

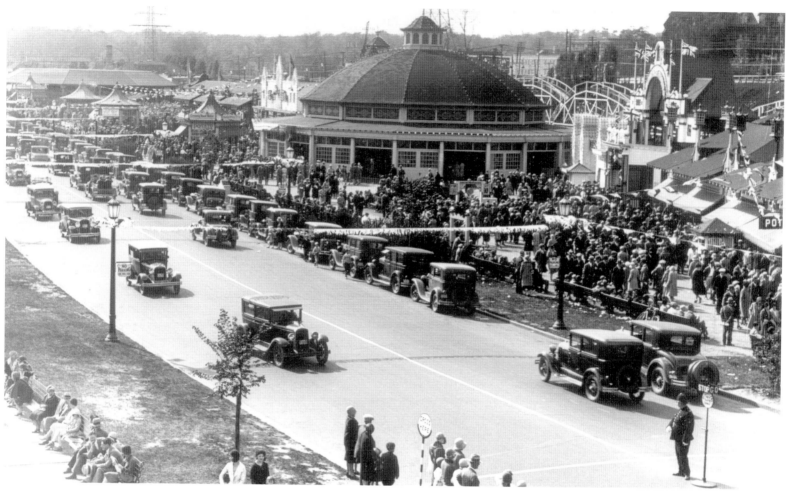

90 Sunnyside Amusement Park

"If you haven't seen Sunnyside Beach, you haven't seen Toronto." So ran the advertisements for almost thirty-five years encouraging young and old to visit "Canada's premier Amusement Park."

Sunnyside was developed by the Toronto Harbour Commission on land once covered by the waters of the old Humber Bay, and was officially opened with suitable ceremony on June 28, 1922. Each summer it became a haven for thousands of Torontonians and visitors to the city who would dine in the Pavilion Restaurant, dance to music of Harry Bedlington and his Whispering Orchestra in the Blue Room, or swim in its heated outdoor pool where Mr. Johnny Walker, the noted swimming instructor, gave free swimming lessons.

In 1932, "The Great Wallendas" from Spain, Vittorio Zacchini "the human cannonball," and "Maybelle's Elephants" thrilled thousands of visitors while they munched "potatoes in a vortex cup," drank O'Keefe's dry ginger ale, and smoked those "smooth as silk" Roxy cigarettes. For years, Easter Parades on the boardwalk and Miss Toronto contests were Sunnyside features. People also flocked to open-air concerts at the Orthophonic Bandshell or to the softball diamond at the east end of the park to watch the ladies of the Oriole, Lakeside, Kodak, and Supreme ball teams give their all.

When the park was permanently closed following the conclusion of the 1955 season, the Flyer roller coaster as well as most of the other rides and amusements were demolished. Nevertheless, a little of Sunnyside lives on at Disneyland in California where several of the horses from Sunnyside's popular Derby Racer continue to frolic.

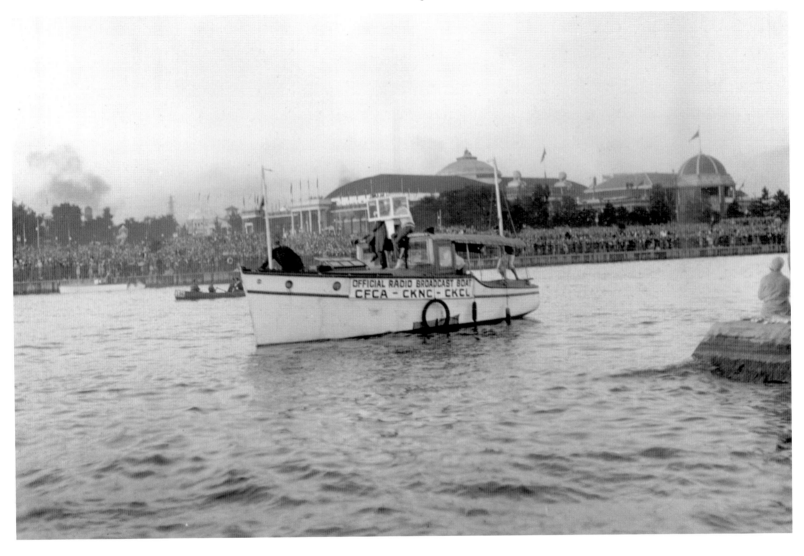

91 At the Canadian National Exhibition, 1929

The first of the CNE's Wrigley Marathon Swims took place in 1927 with the gruelling race held over a twenty-one mile triangular course and open to competitors from all over the world. The first person to win a CNE marathon swim was German-born Ernst Vierkoetter who defeated the local favourite George Young and took home a whopping (for the time) $30,000. The fame of this event was spread far and wide by the broadcast coverage given to it by Toronto's first radio station, the *Toronto Star* newspaper's CFCA, as well as by two other pioneer Toronto stations, CKNC and CKCL. In this photo, reporting on the progress of the 1929 marathon (now reduced to a mere fifteen miles owing to the lack of people completing the original twenty-one mile course) was one of the *Star*'s youthful reporters, Foster Hewitt, who was already enthralling fans with his play-by-play hockey coverage from Mutual Street Area. The 1929 edition of the CNE's popular grandstand show was a pageant entitled "Britannia Muster," and Donald James Baldock was judged the "Grand Champion of the Baby Show."

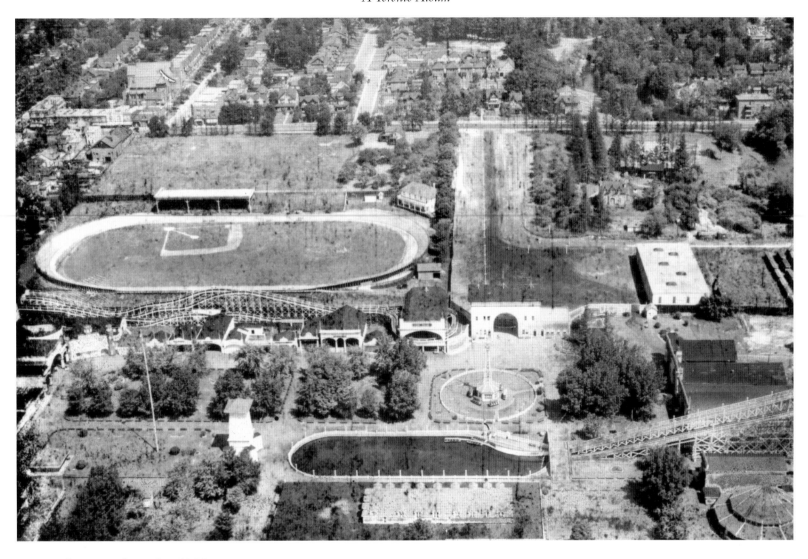

92 Scarboro Beach Park, c1923

Scarboro Beach Park was located south of Queen Street between Maclean and Leuty avenues in the Beach area of the city, and was operated for many years by the Toronto Railway Company. Visitors entered the park under a large wooden archway. To their right was a large grandstand and athletic field where baseball and lacrosse were played. Other attractions included a semi-circular midway, a roller coaster, and a ride called the "Chutes" where for a few pennies one could race down an

incline in a small wooden boat and (with any luck) get drenched in the pool below.

The park was listed as an asset of the TRC, but was not acquired by the TTC following its takeover of the TRC in 1921. The park lingered on for a few years, but closed permanently in 1925.

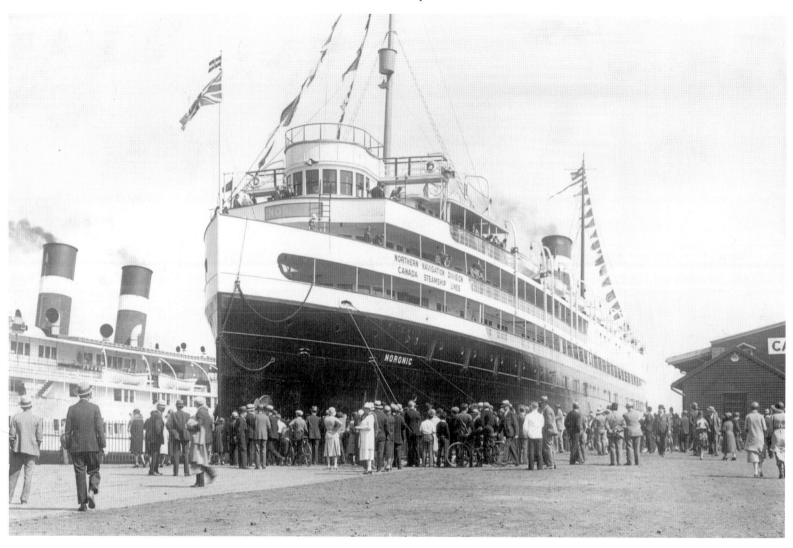

93 S.S. Noronic *in Toronto, 1931*

This photograph shows the steamer *Noronic* during her first visit to the city. Built in 1913 for the Northern Navigation Company (later to become part of Canada Steamship Lines), *Noronic* had six decks and was 362 feet in length making her the largest passenger steamer on the Great Lakes. In summer, she ran cruises from Detroit and Point Edward to Port Arthur and Duluth, and in her off-season from Detroit to the Thousand Islands. The vessel came to a tragic end in Toronto in 1949 when, on an evening stopover in the Port of Toronto during a cruise from Detroit and Cleveland to the Thousand Islands, her berth caught fire at the foot of Yonge Street. A total of 119 perished in the conflagration. Following the disaster, changes to the existing safety regulations forced many other Great Lakes passenger vessels into retirement.

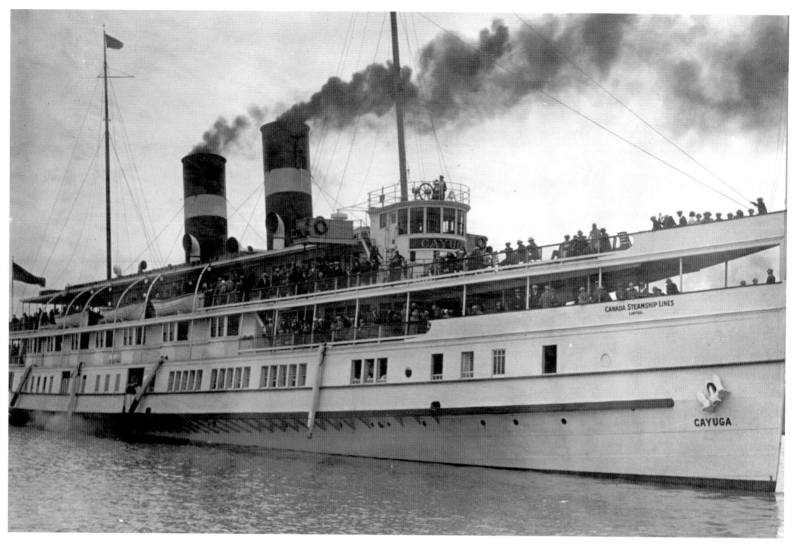

94 S.S. Cayuga

This famous ship, which was launched in 1906 at the Bertram Works near the foot of Bathurst Street, was also built for the Niagara Navigation Company. *Cayuga* sailed from Toronto to Niagara-on-the-Lake and Queenston until 1957 when, for financial reasons, the old vessel was taken reluctantly taken out of service. In 1961, *Cayuga* was dismantled, a mere 1,500 feet away from her birthplace. In her latter years, she had been managed by the Cayuga Steamship Company of which Roland Michener was president and Alan Howard the managing director. Unfortunately, a sailing season of only two or three months was far too short for the company to turn a profit let alone break even. An evening sail across the lake on board *Cayuga* was one of the romantic highlights of Toronto's social life, and her forced retirement left a huge gap in the amenities offered by the city.

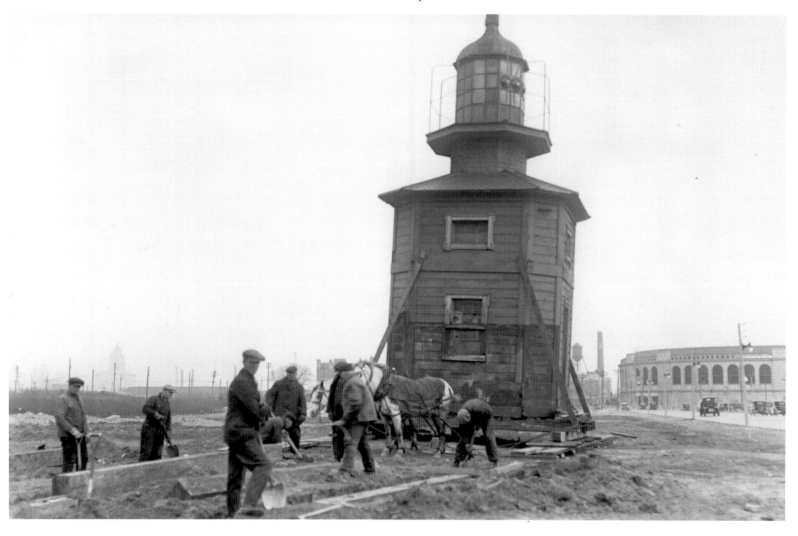

95 Moving the Queen's Wharf lighthouse, 1929

For many years following Simcoe's selection of a site on the north shore of Lake Ontario as the location for a new naval ship yard, the only way into or out of what we now know as Toronto Harbour was via a narrow channel at the west end of the harbour. In the 1830s funds were appropriated to construct a wharf on the mainland side of this channel, a rather flimsy wooden structure that was given the rather grandiose name of the Queen's Wharf.

It soon became obvious that a new western entrance was required further south,

since vessels drawing over 11 feet of water could not navigate the old channel. Over the years, complaints and petitions were presented to various authorities, but it was not until the steamer *Resolute* foundered in the channel in 1906, with the resulting loss of six, that plans for a new entrance were finally given serious consideration.

Actual construction of a new entrance commenced in 1908. The new Western Channel (as it is now called), located 1,300 feet south of the old, opened to navigation

three years later. In 1917, the old channel was filled in by the Toronto Harbour Commission resulting in the lighthouse that stood at the end of the Queen's Wharf left "high and dry." In 1929, it was moved westerly to its present location in front of Molson's Lake Shore Boulevard plant. While its value to mariners is a thing of the past, the structure still possesses historical value revealing to passersby the approximate southerly limit of Toronto's shoreline of more than a century ago.

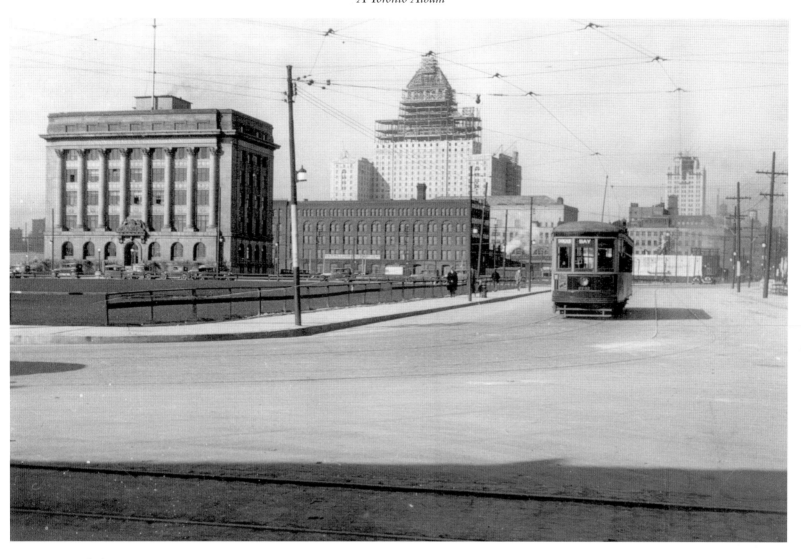

96 Toronto skyline, 1928

All Toronto building records were shattered in 1928. Construction of skyscrapers, such as the Royal York Hotel, the Sterling Bank Tower, and the *Star* building, had brought about a big change in the look of the city's skyline. Apartment buildings erected during 1928 numbered 117 at a total cost of more than $7 million. The Queen's Park Plaza apartment hotel, at the northwest corner of Bloor and Avenue Road, was built for $1 million, the Balmoral apartments at the northeast corner of Avenue Road and Balmoral for $300,000, and the apartments at the southeast corner of St. Clair Avenue and Walmer Road for $110,000. The new Northway Building on Yonge Street was also completed in 1928 as was the Robert Simpson Company's Richmond Street addition and the Electrical Building on the CNE grounds.

Few believed that the boom would ever collapse, but it did following the stock market crash of October 25, 1929. The Great Depression resulted in the Royal York Hotel, the largest in the British Commonwealth, not receiving the business officials had anticipated.

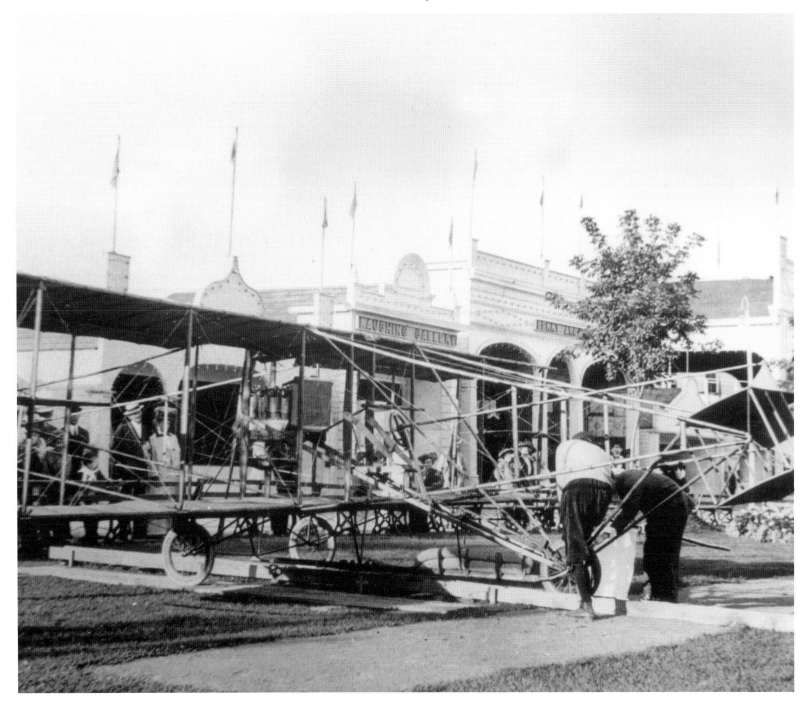

97 Charles Willard and his "Golden Flyer", 1909

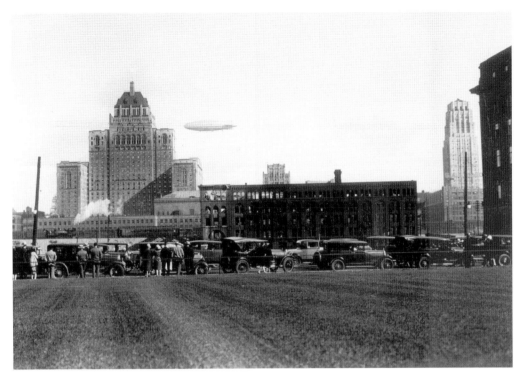

98 The R100 visits Toronto, 1930

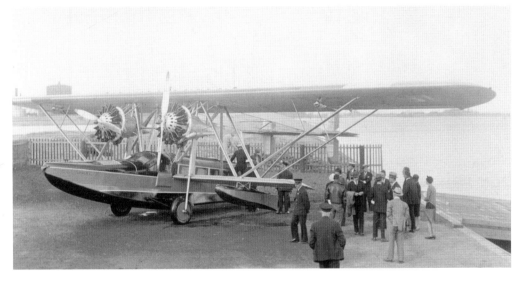

99 Inauguration of Toronto-Buffalo airmail service, the foot of Scott Street, 1929

The Golden Flyer was the name of the flying machine seen here at Scarboro Beach Amusement Park in what was the first advertised flying exhibition held anywhere in North America. American aviator Charles Foster Willard had shipped his plane to the park by train, where he assembled it and successfully took off three times. Landings were a different matter. The first landing was rough enough to require minor repairs be made to the craft. While attempting his second landing, Willard noticed the beach was cluttered with bewildered spectators forcing him to land in the lake. On his third attempt, the biplane's magneto suddenly failed, and once again, Willard and his *Golden Flyer* wound up in Lake Ontario. Willard was a survivor (he died at the age of 94), and so was his flimsy machine. Such a demonstration could hardly have encouraged much confidence in the future of flight.

In 1929, Colonial Airways inaugurated an airmail service between Toronto and Buffalo using a twin-engined Sikorsky S-38 amphibian called the *Nekkah*. The company's Toronto terminal was at what officials termed a "temporary airport" near the foot of Yonge Street. This terminal was closed in 1932.

In 1930, an even more impressive aeronautical visitor stopped by for a visit, the British dirigible R-100 which had just completed its first trans-Atlantic flight. The giant craft had accommodation for 100 passengers and was powered by six gasoline engines. It crossed from England to Montreal in seventy-eight hours; the return flight took fifty-eight hours. Part of the visit to Canada included a side trip to southern Ontario and Toronto where citizens saw the R-100 silhouetted against the year-old Royal York Hotel early in the morning of August 11.

Following the loss of R-101 later that year with the loss of forty-eight lives R-100 was scrapped.

Locally, it would be another nine years before Trans Canada Airlines began flying between Malton Airport and Montreal.

100 Eaton delivery wagon

101 A Canada Bread wagon

102 On the Danforth

Before the internal combustion engine took complete possession of the city streets, horse-drawn vehicles were a common sight well into the 1940s. The horses learned their routes and kept plodding along while the driver delivered his wares. Once in a while, old "Dobbin" would even bring his dozing driver safely back to the depot without any assistance.

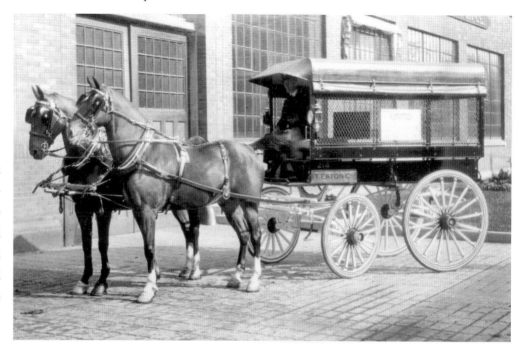

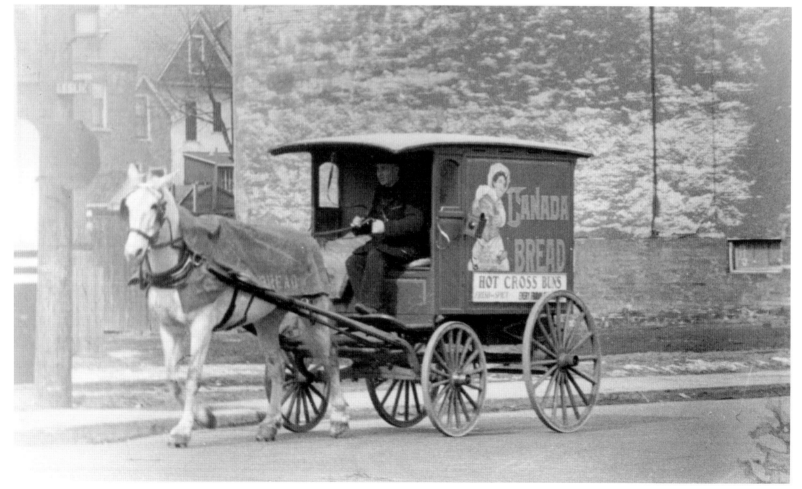

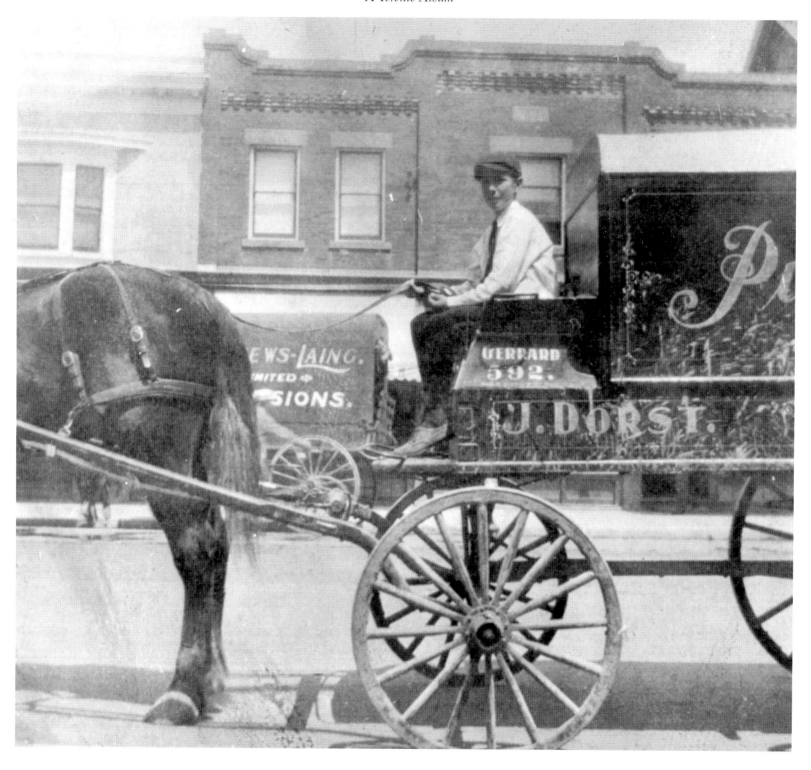

To celebrate the city's 100th anniversary, a colourful evening pageant was presented at the mammoth CNE Grandstand on July 2, 3 and 4, 1934. Titled "Milestones of a Century," the spectacular consisted of twelve distinct episodes that featured more than 3,500 participants.

Episode No. 1: The Governor Simcoe Branch United Empire Loyalists, The Canadian Order of Foresters. When the young American colonies became victorious in their war with Great Britain, many who wished to remain loyal to the Monarch found themselves homeless. Determined to live under the flag of Great Britain many made the move north to Canada. The loyal Six Nation Indians precede them, and as the action proceeds the Six Nation Indians are discovered being welcomed by four British officers and directed to their new lands, which thereafter will be their home. The officers then return to welcome the Loyalists who proceed to draw lots for their land.

Episode No. 2: The Canadian Order of Oddfellows, The Shriners Drill Corp, The Patrol, Rameses Temple, A.A. O.H.M.S. Arrival of Governor Simcoe: Col John Graves Simcoe, the first Lieutenant-Governor of Upper Canada, crossed Lake Ontario in May, 1793 and began preparations for the construction of the Town of York.

The Episode opens with the arrival on the stage of a detachment of Queen's Rangers. They are followed by Mrs. Simcoe and the children and a guard of sailors from the ship. Governor Simcoe arrives with his Council and greets his family. As Col Simcoe, Mrs. Simcoe and the children turn to leave, the Queen's Rangers form again and march off.

Episode No. 3: The United Church Young People's Association. The villagers of the little town of York are pursuing their peaceful ways when suddenly a courier arrives with the stirring news that Admiral Horatio Nelson has met and destroyed the French Mediterranean fleet in Aboukir Bay.

The excitement grows. More people rush from their homes to hear the glad tidings. A small cannon is hauled down the stage and a salute fired. Casks of ale are broached as the populace fittingly celebrates the great event.

Episode No. 4: The Independent Order of Foresters Brock and the York Militia: As the light increases, General Brock is discovered in the centre of a group of men, telling them of the new danger that has arisen, and that the country is in under the threat of attack by American troops at any moment. The men respond with a cheer, and prepare to go forth under the able leadership of the hero of Upper Canada. As this group marches back the lights fade, and in the moment of darkness the trained Militia march in their place. General Brock's great efforts have been rewarded and he and his men go forth to victory.

Episode No. 5: The Anglican Young People's Association Capture of York: On a pleasant morning in April, 1813, an American fleet makes a sudden appearance and proceeds to attack the fort. Their objective is the destruction of a ship that is in the process of construction. The regulars, aided gallantly by the Militia, make a brave stand, but being terribly out-numbered by the Americans, are forced to retreat. They burn the ship to prevent if falling into the hands of the enemy and proceed in orderly retreat through the town. The Americans press on and into the Fort. As they do so, a magazine blows up, killing General Pike and two hundred men. Another group of Americans appears, under the command of General Dearborn, and proceeds to burn the town. Bishop Strachan makes violent protest in vain and the episode ends with the town in flames.

Episode No. 6: The Native Sons of Canada William Lyon Mackenzie: The Tableau stage slowly lights to a symbolic picture of the election of William Lyon Mackenzie as first Mayor of Toronto. As the light begins to dim, the stage action begins. W.L. Mackenzie is discovered being drawn in his carriage by his enthusiastic admirers, who have dispensed with horses in the high fever of election excitement. The first Mayor greets them with a wave of his hat, but the excitement of the crowd rises to a high pitch and they pull him from the carriage and carry him on their shoulders. He is brought back again, placed in his carriage, and makes a triumphant exit.

Episode No. 7: The County Orange Lodge. The scene changes. Discontent has grown in the northern settlements until the blacksmiths are forging pikes, and Mackenzie is advocating a march on Toronto and the overthrow of the Government by force of arms. The rebels have reached Montgomery's Tavern when the alarm bells start to ring. People rush on the stage in great excitement. Col Fitzgibbon appears and quickly lines up his force of old Home Guardsmen, and prepares to march against the aroused farmers. Just as they are about to move off, a courier arrives on horseback. The militia has the situation in hand, and the rebels are dispersed. The happy populace lines up and cheers as the active militia march past.

Episode No. 8: Young Women's Christian Association, Young Men's Christian Association, Eaton Young Men's Club The Royal ball: The Ball at Osgoode Hall in honour of His Royal Highness, the Prince of Wales, proved to be a gala event. The scene opens with the old-time waltz already in progress. As the dance finishes, the arrival of His Royal Highness is announced. The Prince proceeds to the raised dais in the centre of the stage. Mr. Cameron of the Queen's Bench approaches the Prince and requests the honour of his signature on the scroll of the Lawyer's Society. The Prince kindly acquiesces and signs the scroll. The Duke of Newcastle, his courtly keeper, then introduces the future King to his first dancing partner and the band strikes up the Minuet. The dance finishes, the clock strikes twelve, and the young Prince proceeds to take his leave as the band plays "Auld Lang Syne."

Episode No. 9: The Toronto Fire Department, The Baptist Young People's Association, De La Salle "Oakland" Semi-Centennial, 1884: In 1884, when Alderman McMurrich proposed a Semi-Centennial celebration, the idea caught the imagination of the people. Among many of the features of the celebration was the Parade. Beginning with the Civic Council on foot, the Parade consists of a float, "The Occupation of the British," followed by the band. Then the float, "Landing of Governor Simcoe," followed by the Toronto Bicycle Club. The Parade of the Firemen concludes the day's celebration.

Episode No. 10: The Gentlemen of the Anglican Young People's Association, The Gentlemen of the United Church Young People's Association Queen Victoria's funeral: The death and funeral of a great and noble queen is symbolized with the simplicity and beauty that marked her life.

Episodes Nos. 11 and 12: The entire Personnel Armistice Day and the introduction of the great Choir, who sing the songs of the wartime era.

The return to peace and optimism toward the future is reached in the Choir's rendition of Sir Edward Elgar's great work, "The Epilogue from Caractacus." GOD SAVE THE KING

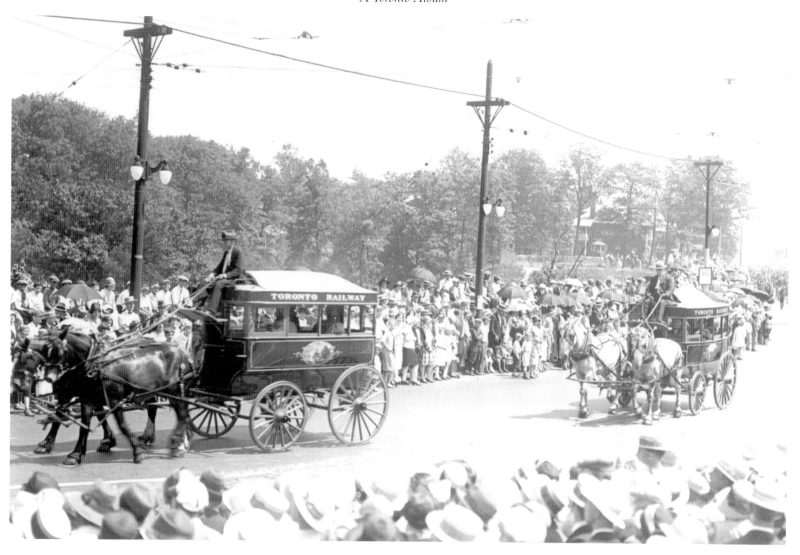

103 Centennial Parade, 1934

In 1934, Toronto celebrated its 100th anniversary as a city. Among the festivities was this parade, passing along Bloor Street near Parliament. An old omnibus of the Toronto Street Railway, suitably refurbished, was an eye catcher. It was painted green, sat six passengers, and ran on routes which were not travelled enough to support an investment in street railway track.

March 5 was the last day of Toronto's first century, and a vast watch-night service was held in the Coliseum at the CNE grounds. Mackenzie King was present, along with other dignitaries, a crowd of 11,000, and a choir of 2,500. The first part of the service was "devoted to thanksgiving and praise of the Lord for his bounty," and the president of the university preached on a text from Isaiah: "Enlarge the place of thy tent and let them stretch forth the curtains of thine habitations; spare not, lengthen thy cords and strengthen thy stakes." Outside were fireworks, "bombs," and a bonfire on the Island organized by the Harbour Commission. Toronto's "Big Ben" boomed in the new century. Everyone in the Coliseum stood to listen to the choir sing Stanford's "Te Deum" and the Hallelujah chorus, and then joined in "God Save the King." That event was followed later that summer by a mammoth spectacular at the CNE Grandstand.

104 Gladys Marie Smith
at the Grand, 1925

Toronto's first Grand Opera House was erected in 1874 on the south side of Adelaide Street just west of Yonge. Its first play presented at the new theatre was "School for Scandal," which was performed before the Governor-General. The Grand Opera House was destroyed by fire in 1879. The structure shown in the accompanying photo was opened on the site of the old the following year.

On the theatre marquee appears the name of the undisputed "Queen of the Silent Screen," Mary Pickford. Mary was actually born Gladys Marie Smith in 1893, in a small house at 211 University Avenue in downtown Toronto. Certainly, an unpretentious start for the young Torontonian who would become known all over the world as "America's sweetheart."

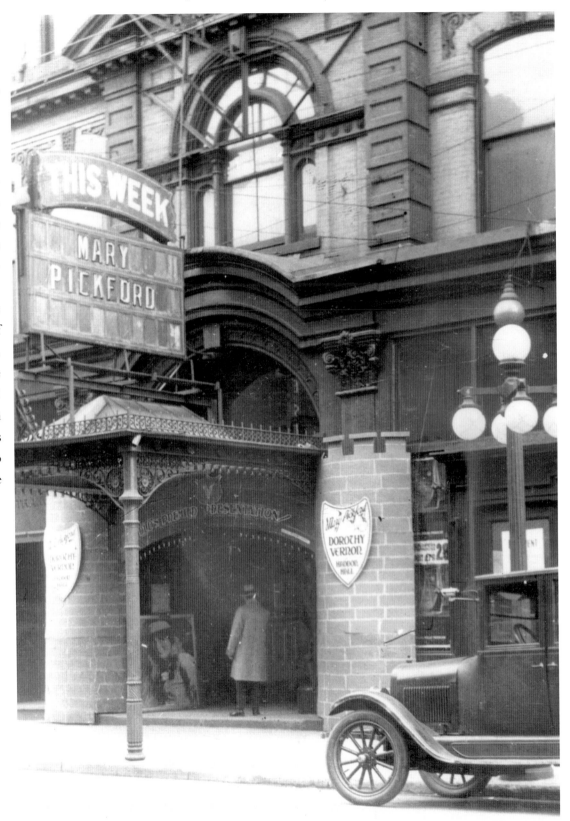

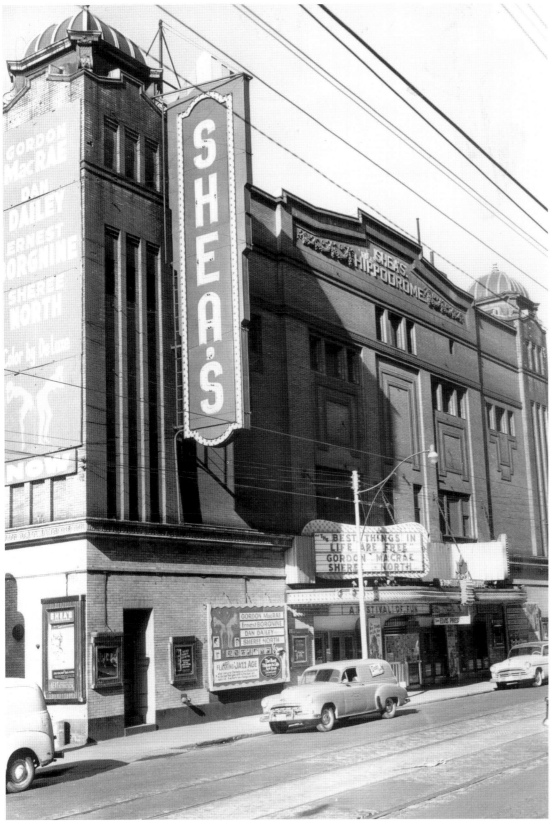

105 Shea's Hippodrome, 1941

Jeremiah Shea's Hippodrome on Terauley (later Bay) Street was one of Toronto's largest theatres. It seated 3,663 people, showed vaudeville acts, silent and talking movies, and was famous for its mighty pipe organ (subsequently relocated to Casa Loma). The Hippodrome was demolished in 1957 and the site cleared for Nathan Phillips Square and the new City Hall.

In early 1930, Torontonians seeking an entertaining night out could hear Sir Harry Lauder in person at the Royal Alexandra, see and hear Rudy Vallee, the radio idol of millions, in an "all-talking, singing, dancing comedy-drama 'The Vagabond Lover'" at the Pantages theatre (where Radio Pictures' famous dancing girls were also featured) or thrill to Ramon Novarro and Dorothy Jordan, "the erstwhile Broadway charmer," in "Devil May Care," at the Tivoli. In this motion picture, Novarro plays a "dashing young lieutenant in Bonaparte's army who is condemned to death, evades the firing squad by leaping over the wall against which they have placed him for his last stand against fate and secretes himself in the bedchamber of the most beautiful young girl in France."

The Pantages theatre is now the Canon theatre.

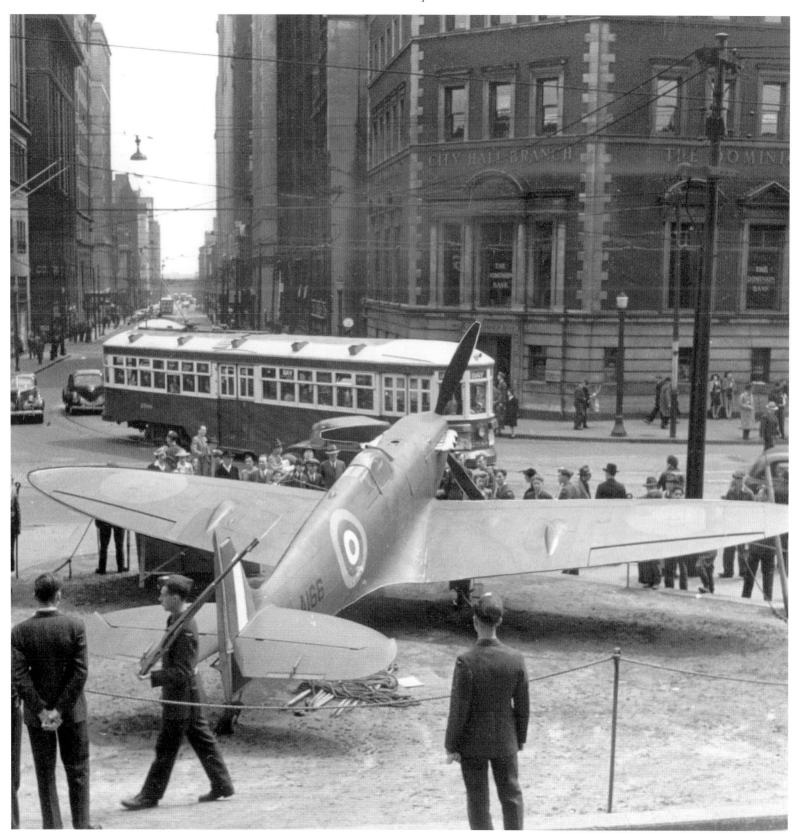

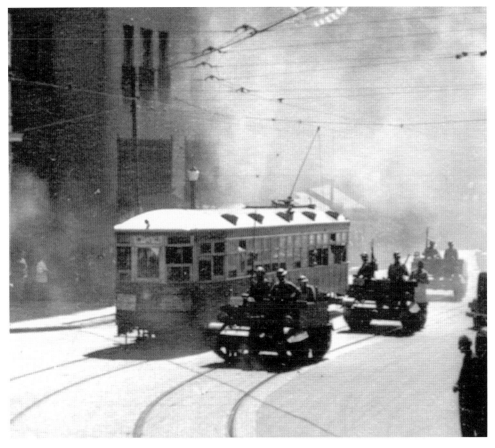

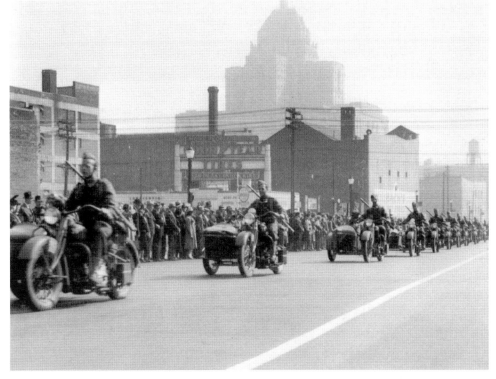

106 A Spitfire in front of City Hall

107 Bren-gun carriers on Bay Street

108 A parade on University Avenue

Canada entered the Second World War on September 10, 1939. Toronto provided men, women, and money, suffered some privation through rationing, and once again witnessed rapid wartime development of many of its industries. At the same time, consideration was being given to the amalgamation of Toronto with its surrounding municipalities, some of which had become bankrupt during the years of the Great Depression. These outlying communities contained an increasing percentage of Toronto's workers and its factories. The seeds of a metropolitan form of government had been sown. A severe housing problem began to develop as well, and soon the city began to envision more and more apartment buildings replacing old family houses. The devastation and slow recovery of both Britain and Europe caused a wave of immigrants to arrive in the city, gradually eroding the British-American character of the place and giving it the new, more cosmopolitanism character of a world city.

By this time, as far as this book is concerned, Toronto was more and more recognizable as the central city we have today. We shall end here, confident that for the next thirty years most of its citizens lived in reasonable happiness, leading productive, tolerant, honest, sporting, and enterprising lives, as had Torontonians of earlier generations. There will also be problems in the functioning of the ever larger and more complex environment of the city as its citizens and their government try to make it a better place.

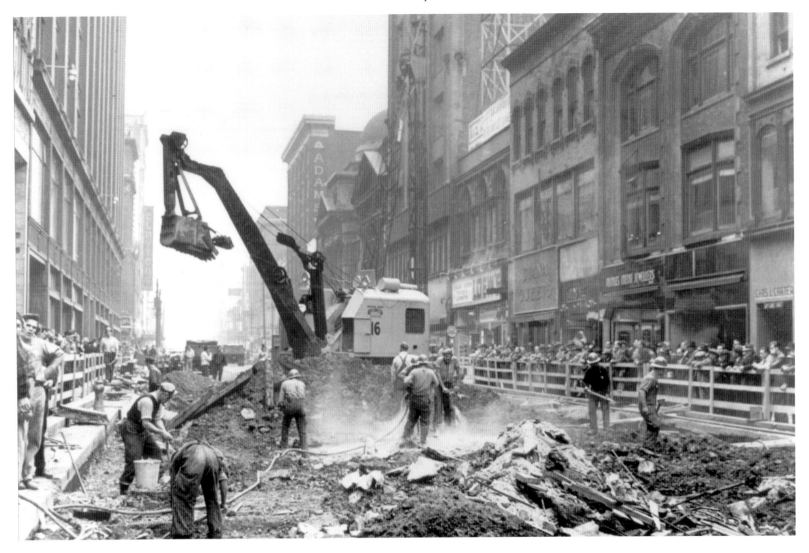

109 Tearing up Yonge Street for the subway, 1950

The old Eaton store is on the left of the photo, while on the right are such well known Toronto enterprises as Diana Sweets restaurant, Loew's, theatre and, up the street at the Shuter Street corner, Adams Furniture's main store.

References

Sources for text quotations accompanying the following photographs:

1 *75 Years, 1848-1923,* Consumers' Gas Company of Toronto, p.23.

4 C.P. Mulvany, *Toronto: Past and Present,* Toronto, 1884 (1971), pp. 44, 291.

12 G. Mercer Adam, *Illustrated Toronto,* Montreal, 1891, p.59.

12 The *Globe,* July 5, 1888.

15 *Cab and Livery By-Laws,* Police Commissioners, 1891 ed.

15 J. Ross Robertson, *Landmarks of Toronto,* Toronto, 1895. From the *Empire,* quoted in C.S. Clark, *Of Toronto the Good,* Montreal, 1898; Toronto, 1970, pp. 93-5.

17 Quoted in Henry Roxborough, *One Hundred – Not Out,* Toronto, 1866, p. 41.

19 Programme of the Third International Epworth League Convention in Toronto, July, 1897.

20 Mulvany, *Toronto: Past and Present,* pp. 81, 79.

22 Mulvany, *Toronto: Past and Present,* pp. 148, 144-5.

26 J.E. Middleton, *The Municipality of Toronto,* Toronto, New York, 1923, pp. 345-5.

27 Middleton, *The Municipality of Toronto,* p. 362.

31 Louis H. Pursley, *Street Railways of Toronto, 1861-1921,* Los Angeles, 1958.

42 *Toronto as Seen from the Trolley Car,* TRC, 1894.

45 *Toronto: A City of Beautiful Homes,* Toronto, n.d.

53 Middleton, *The Municipality of Toronto,* pp. 354-5.

55 *Toronto Annual,* 1917 ed.

70,71 *Souvenir of Toronto,* Gray Coach Lines, 1925.

89 *Toronto at a Glance,* Bureau of Municipal Research, 1929.

90 *Sunnyside Beach Preview,* 1932.

Other useful books about the city include:

Eric Arthur, *Toronto: No Mean City,* Toronto, 1964.

Harry Bruce, *The Short Happy Walks of Max Macpherson,* Toronto, 1968.

R. Correli, *The Toronto That Used To Be,* Toronto, 1964.

John F. Due, *The Intercity Electric Railway Industry in Canada,* Toronto, 1966.

J. Clarence Duff, *Pen Sketches of Historic Toronto,* Toronto, 1967.

Edwin C. Guillet, *Pioneer Inns and Taverns,* Toronto, 1964.

D.C. Masters, *The Rise of Toronto,* Toronto, 1947.

J.E. Middleton, *Toronto's Hundred Years,* Toronto, 1934.

Louis H. Pursley, *The TTC Story,* Los Angeles, 1961.

Toronto Year Books.

Bruce West, *Toronto,* Toronto, 1967.